Developing
Professional Skills:
Criminal Procedure

Renée McDonald Hutchins

Jacob A. France Professor of Public Interest Law
and Co-Director, Clinical Law Program
University of Maryland Carey School of Law

Series Editor: Colleen Medill

WEST
ACADEMIC
PUBLISHING

© 2017 LEG, Inc. d/b/a West Academic
    444 Cedar Street, Suite 700
    St. Paul, MN 55101
    1-877-888-1330
West, West Academic Publishing, and West Academic are trademarks of West Publishing Corporation, used under license.

Printed in the United States of America

ISBN: 978-1-63460-277-8

To the Hemphills

Preface

LAW SCHOOLS TODAY ASPIRE more consistently than in years past to teach professional legal skills. The current emphasis on skills training is a response to the criticism that the traditional law school curriculum does not adequately train students to practice law. In recent years, the high cost of law school tuition coupled with the tight job market has intensified the demand for more skills training in law schools.

Notwithstanding the demand for (and desire to do) more, incorporating skills training into doctrinal courses can be challenging. Simulations that are too straightforward are easy to administer, but may be of little pedagogical value because they do not imitate the intricacies of practice. On the other hand, excessively elaborate simulations may crowd out customary coverage of legal concepts and doctrines—leaving both the professor and the students frustrated. The goal is simulations that are carefully constructed to work within the time and resource constraints of a traditional doctrinal course. Such simulations are a valuable addition.

This book seeks to provide an array of carefully constructed exercises that range from the very direct to the relatively more complex. Students are expected to spend an average of one or two hours outside of the classroom preparing the skills assignments for each chapter. And, even the most complicated assignment in the book can be completed in no more than three hours. Moreover, as explained in detail in the Teacher's Manual, more complex assignments can be easily scaled down (or broken up into multiple assignments) to provide a more streamlined learning experience.

Developing Professional Skills: Criminal Procedure is designed to provide skills training to law students in a substantively-targeted and time-efficient manner. Each chapter in this book focuses on one or more of the following four core legal skills:

- Client Counseling (including new client engagement, interviewing, fact gathering, and advice delivery);

- Legal Drafting (including client correspondence and correspondence with opposing counsel through letters and emails, as well as drafting of traditional legal documents);

- Negotiation; and

- Advocacy

The professor may choose to provide students with the electronic templates for assignments that are included in the comprehensive Teacher's Manual. These templates give students some direction with regard to formatting. The templates are also one method for allowing students to complete and submit assignments electronically.

The Teacher's Manual gives the professor both guidance and discretion in determining how much classroom discussion time to devote to the material in each chapter. The professor may spend a brief amount of time reviewing the answer to the problem presented in the chapter. Alternatively, the professor may expand the discussion to include concepts of professional responsibility and the norms of modern legal practice. Suggestions for incorporating professional responsibility concepts and the norms of legal practice into the classroom discussion are contained in the Teacher's Manual. For professors who wish to expand the scope of a skills exercise, selected provisions of the Model Rules of Professional Conduct are reproduced in the Appendix material at the end of the book.

Developing Professional Skills: Criminal Procedure is intended to bring to life the material taught in a basic Criminal Procedure course. For that reason, the exercises included in this book are generally organized to track those topics that are typically covered in such a course. While the standard law school routine of reading cases and answering questions helps students learn the substantive material, encouraging students to actively engage that same material in simulation encourages deeper comprehension and longer-term retention. As attorneys, students may encounter idiosyncratic, demanding, and occasionally unreasonable clients; constantly evolving technology; old-fashioned financial and time-management constraints; and most of all, problems to solve. They will then be asked to craft (or help craft) responses to these challenges. Although no book can truly mimic the nuanced tapestry that is modern legal practice, the skills exercises in this book can be used to enhance and enrich the students' educational experience. This enhancement and enrichment will help students move closer to becoming practicing lawyers and legal counselors.

In closing, thanks go first to Professor Colleen Medill at the University of Nebraska College of Law for being the guiding force behind the *Developing Professional Skills* series. Thanks also go to the talented editors at West Academic for giving me an opportunity to be part of the Developing series. I also must express my appreciation to my colleagues at the University of Maryland Carey School of Law, and my writing-partners-in-crime at the Mid-Atlantic Criminal Law Research Collective for their time and guidance. Finally, my eternal thanks go to my Criminal Procedure students who endured early versions of some of these exercises; and my fabulous former research assistants, Meg Raker and Abby Metzger, for their cheerful willingness to always "find everything."

—Renée McDonald Hutchins

Introduction

DEVELOPING PROFESSIONAL SKILLS: CRIMINAL PROCEDURE
introduces you to a variety of skills that are regularly engaged by
experienced legal practitioners. Like any type of skill, acquiring professional legal skills takes time and patience; but most of all, it takes
practice. Each chapter in this book provides you with the opportunity
to practice a legal skill that you are likely to use again and again after
you graduate from law school.

The chapters of this book are organized to coincide with topics that
usually are covered in a basic Criminal Procedure class. In Chapter
One, you are asked to draft an introductory email to a potential client.
In the exercise you will navigate the sometimes tricky space between
generating new business and realistically advising a client on the
likely chance of success. In Chapter Two, you are assigned to interview
a new client. The client has been charged with a violent murder in
what appears to be an open and shut case of guilt. But, is there more to
the case than meets the eye? In Chapter Three, you will draft a letter
counseling a client on the relative strength of various legal claims.
In Chapter Four, you will write a retainer letter. Your professor may
also ask you to construct the outline of your suppression strategy in
the case. In Chapter Five, you will build upon the lessons learned in
Chapter Four by drafting an actual suppression motion for a client
arrested on murder charges. In Chapter Six, you will move from a
suppression motion to a suppression hearing. In this chapter, you
work in role as a junior prosecutor to prepare the direct examination
of a police officer who will be the government's primary witness at the
suppression hearing. In Chapter Seven, you are again assigned in role
as a prosecutor. This time, you are asked to approve a plea offer that
has been negotiated by one of the junior attorneys in your office. In
considering the appropriate plea offer, you are asked to evaluate the

strength of the government's case and the relative defenses that might exist. In Chapter Eight, you will be assigned to draft a strategy memo for your supervisor in connection with a politically sensitive case the office is thinking about prosecuting. In Chapter Nine, you move back into the role of defense attorney to draft the argument section of an appellate brief. In the final chapter, Chapter Ten, you will make an oral argument. If you were assigned Chapter Nine, your professor may ask you to present an oral argument in Chapter Ten based upon your own research and writing. Alternatively, you may be asked to use the briefs provided in Chapter Ten as the springboard for your oral argument.

Client interviewing, client counseling, legal research and writing, negotiating, and advocacy are the core skills of the legal profession. *Developing Professional Skills: Criminal Procedure* provides you with an opportunity to begin to cultivate these skills.

Finally, many of the police records and other "official" documents contained in this workbook are based on public records in actual cases. The names of all parties (and some of the underlying details) have been changed to protect identities.

Table of Contents

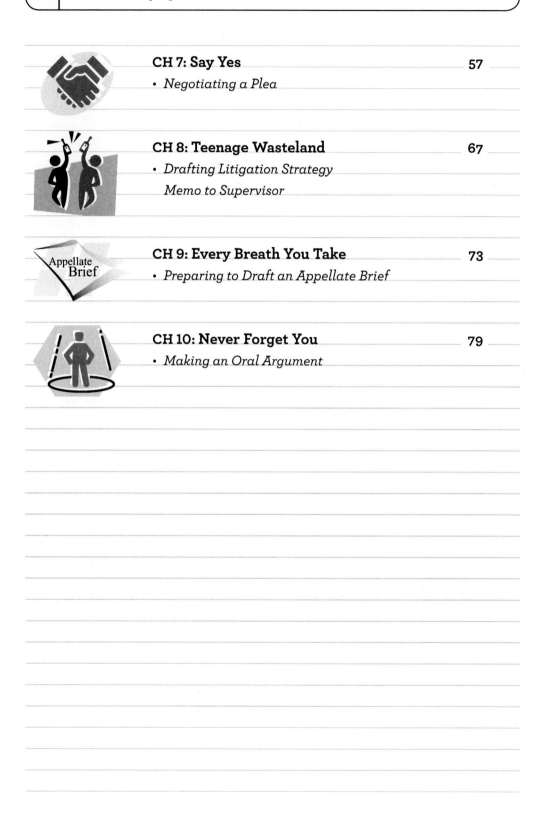

Developing Professional Skills:

CRIMINAL PROCEDURE

CHAPTER 1

Hello
Drafting an Introductory Email

YOU ARE SOLO PRACTITIONER with a practice that specializes in traffic and low-level criminal cases. You have been doing a decent job of paying the bills, but you aren't yet in a position to turn down cases. You really do need all the business you can get!

Earlier this morning, you received a call from a young woman looking for a lawyer. She has been charged with possessing a weapon and the case is going to trial in a month.

Your notes of the phone call are below:

> Young woman, Jenna Douglas ("JD"), 23 y/o, no prior record. JD was shopping in mall. Asked sales clerk to show her a designer watch. Clerk gave JD watch, left to help another customer. JD looked at watch. Was too expensive ($1300!). After several minutes, JD put watch on counter, waved to clerk, and left store.
>
> A few minutes later—JD walking in mall; is approached by mall security guard. Security guard said sales clerk reported a stolen watch. JD explained she put watch on counter and left store. Security guard asked JD to return to store with him. JD agreed.

Back in store, clerk accused JD of stealing watch. JD insisted she put watch on counter. "I didn't steal anything."

JD began to walk out of store. Sales clerk instructed security guard to "hold" JD while clerk called police. Guard grabbed JD by shoulder; forcibly pushed her against counter. With other hand, officer frisked JD's outer clothing. Officer felt a hard object in JD's waistband. Reached in, retrieved 8-inch long hunting knife from a sheath clipped to JD's pants. Watch was not found.

JD explained: "knife is my dad's. We've been watching a lot of "The Walking Dead" lately. You never know when the zombie apocalypse is coming. I know it was stupid ... but I like to feel prepared."

Police arrived at store minutes after guard found knife. Guard gave police officers the knife. JD handcuffed by police and arrested (possession of a dangerous weapon). Police thanked guard for "preventing another incident."

Criminal case (weapons possession) going to trial next month. JD wants prosecution to go away quickly; is "irate" and "pissed off" she was accused of stealing. Was talking to friend who said, "Search was obviously illegal." Friend says suppress knife, criminal case will go away. JD wants you to make that happen. Wants email confirming representation and suppression strategy.

Email = JDouglas@client.com

After hanging up the phone, you go over your notes. On the one hand you could really use the business. On the other hand, if you're assessing the case honestly, you don't think there is any basis for suppressing the knife. But then you think, "If by some stroke of genius I can get the knife suppressed/excluded, the prosecution won't have a case!"

Draft an email to the client assessing the case and informing her 1) whether you will accept representation in the criminal case, 2) the potential claims you will raise (at the suppression hearing and beyond), and 3) the obstacles you see to suppressing the knife.

 ## Points to Consider:

1. Making Contact: This will be your first written communication with a potential client. The client has asked you to use a relatively informal mode of communication—email. But, in drafting your response, consider the fact that this is your initial written contact with the client. Are there reasons to balance the relative informality of the preferred communication method with greater formality in terms of substance?

2. Application of the Fourth Amendment: In thinking about the likelihood of suppression/exclusion, consider first whether the Fourth Amendment even applies. Are there additional facts that you need to make that assessment? If so, what are they? Will you inform the client of the need for this additional information? Why? Why not?

3. Cash vs. Credibility: The potential client has told you she wants the case to "go away." She has talked to a friend who has convinced her suppression is possible. She is also emotional about her treatment, saying she is "irate" and "pissed off" at the clerk and the guard. If you promise to do what she asks, she will certainly sign you up as her attorney and you will be able to generate fees for the case. But, the facts, as you now understand them, don't appear to present a viable case for suppression. Should you start now to readjust the client's expectations? Why? If so, how can you manage the client's expectations without losing the new business?

CHAPTER 2

Janie's Got a Gun

Client Interviewing

YOU ARE ENROLLED IN the criminal defense clinic at your law school. The clinic engages in "vertical representation of clients," a representation model in which clients are represented by a single attorney through all stages of their criminal case from arraignment to sentencing. In keeping with this method of representation, students in the clinic do intake interviews and, if the client is accepted, students work with an attorney on the client's case for the entire semester.

You were working intake late last week and received the paperwork for a woman who was recently arrested for first-degree murder. Despite the clinic's best efforts, bail was not set in the case and the woman is being held at the local jail awaiting trial. Your supervisor in the clinic has asked you to go out to interview the woman to get her side of the story. Once you have her version of events, you can construct an investigation strategy, and can begin to explore potential defenses. Depending on what she says, you may also explore early plea options. You have several reports from the police file (attached). You expect many more documents will be turned over in discovery later in the case. But for now, you at least have a summary of what some witnesses have told the police, as well as the prosecution's basic understanding of the facts surrounding the crime

The client's name is Janie Welch. She is a 20 y/o single mother who suffers from drug addiction. The victim in the case is a 65 y/o man named Clyde McFadden. Janie was working as McFadden's caretaker, cook, and housekeeper while McFadden recovered from prostate  cancer. After accepting his job offer, Janie moved in with McFadden at his request. McFadden was found dead in his trailer late one evening. Welch is the one who reported his death. McFadden died of gunshot wounds to his back and blunt force trauma to his head.

Before you go to interview Welch, your supervisor would like to see your written interview strategy. This document may take the form of a list of specific questions you will ask, or may be a more general outline of the areas or topics you plan to cover. Once your plan is approved, you will go out to conduct the interview. When you return, you will debrief with your supervisor, including a review of what you learned from Ms. Welch. In particular, your supervisor will be keen to know whether additional investigation (expert or factual) will be critical; and if so, with regard to what issues.

Police File

CRIMINAL INVESTIGATION REPORT POLICE DEPARTMENT		1. General Broadcast? NO	2. COMPLAINT CONTROL NO. 05408176
3. TYPE OF REPORT Crime against person	4. INITIAL OR FOLLOW-UP Initial	5. COMPLAINT/ VICTIM'S NAME (Last, First, M.I.) MCFADDEN, Clyde P.	
	6. PAGE 1	7. CRIME/ INCIDENT Shooting/Homicide	
8. COMPLAINANT/WITNESS Welch, Janie Ann	9. SEX /RACE F/W	10. LOCATION OF CRIME interior of private trailer	

12. NARRATIVE: RECORD YOUR ACTIVITY AND ALL DEVELOPMENTS IN THIS CASE. INCLUDE ADDITIONAL VICTIMS WITNESSES AND SUSPECTS AS OUTLINED ABOVE. DESCRIBE DETAILS OF INCIDENT. DESCRIBE EVIDENCE AND PROPERTY AND INDICATE DISPOSITION.

Culprit broke into dwelling, shot victim and stole. Scene was processed for fingerprints and was photographed. Prints were found on weapons (rifle and brick) and at scene. Property stolen was a color television set, a vacuum cleaner, and an unknown quantity of drugs. Complainant was interviewed by myself and Officer Downing(notes attached).

MODE OF OPERATION: Culprit(s) threw a brick through the rear, east side window of the victim's trailer. Then the culprit reached through the broken glass and raised the lower portion of the trailer window. After cutting or tearing the screen on the lower half of the window, culprit entered through opened window. Once inside, for reasons yet unknown, culprit obtained .22 caliber rifle kept inside of trailer and used it to shoot victim more than once in back. At some point later, culprit used same rifle to club victim's head, crushing skull. Prior to leaving culprit stole several items.

13. CRIME LAB TECH. Butler		14. CLASSIFICATION Pending		
15. INITIAL INVESTIGATOR I.D. NUMBER Linc Alton 0041		16. STATUS Open	17. REFERRED	18. TELETYPE NO.

NARRATIVE:

On Tuesday at 2040 hrs. I arrived at the Mid-way Market (located on Naylor and Jersey Road). As I stepped out of my vehicle, Miss Welch (victim's live-in caretaker) and Mr. Wilson (Miss Welch's boyfriend) approached me and advised Clyde McFadden (the victim) was lying on the floor of his residence and was seriously hurt. Meanwhile Mr. Burns (Mr. Wilson's roommate) was telephoning the barrack to advise of same situation. I transported Miss Welch in my vehicle to the victim's residence while Mr. Burns and Mr. Wilson used their vehicles. While en route, Miss Welch advised me she left the victim home alone at 1800 hrs and returned around 2000 hrs. She then went to Mr. Wilson's residence on Cabin Road. Mr. Wilson, Mr. Burns and Welch then went to the victim's residence where they discovered the victim lying on the living room floor. They then went to the Mid-way Market to call the police.

Upon arrival at the victim's residence, Mr. Burns and I went into the residence and the victim appeared to be deceased. Miss Welch and Mr. Wilson remained outside the residence. The barrack was notified and advised me to secure the scene. The barrack also advised an ambulance was en route and that Sgt. Alton was also en route. While waiting for assistance Miss Welch advised that the front door had been locked with a padlock by her when she left at 1800 hrs. Mr. Burns and I examined the rear of the residence and discovered a window on the side of trailer had been broken.

Sgt. Alton arrived and the case was turned over to him.

Ofc. Downing, #0856

CRIMINAL INVESTIGATION REPORT POLICE DEPARTMENT		1. General Broadcast? NO	2. COMPLAINT CONTROL NO. 05408176
3. TYPE OF REPORT Crime against person	4. INITIAL OR FOLLOW-UP Follow-Up(1)	5. COMPLAINT/ VICTIM'S NAME (Last, First, M.I.) MCFADDEN, Clyde P.	
	6. PAGE 1	7. CRIME/ INCIDENT Shooting/Homicide	
8. COMPLAINANT/WITNESS suspect Welch, Janie Ann	9. SEX /RACE F/W	10. LOCATION OF CRIME interior of private trailer	

12. NARRATIVE: RECORD YOUR ACTIVITY AND ALL DEVELOPMENTS IN THIS CASE. INCLUDE ADDITIONAL VICTIMS WITNESSES AND SUSPECTS AS OUTLINED ABOVE. DESCRIBE DETAILS OF INCIDENT. DESCRIBE EVIDENCE AND PROPERTY AND INDICATE DISPOSITION:

Arrived at scene at 2130 hours to assist with the investigation of a reported homicide.

Initial survey disclosed victim lying in the living room face down and head toward the TV, which was on and loud. To the rear of the trailer on the northeast side was a broken window which lead into the master bedroom. An unbroken storm window was on the floor and leaning against the bed directly below the broken window. The entire area was photographed.

Near the middle of the trailer at a point where the hall begins, several live .22 caliber L/R bullets were located along with several spent casings and one projectile. These were all collected and located on a crime scene sketch, and packaged for future identification.

Funeral home arrived at scene and removed victim to morgue where medical examiner ordered autopsy. Corporal on scene located a broken rifle behind an outbuilding to the rear of the trailer. The stock was broken into two pieces and had what appeared to be blood and hair on it.

Cause of death: gunshot wounds to rear torso; blunt force trauma to head.

15. INITIAL INVESTIGATOR I.D. NUMBER Linc Alton 0041	16. STATUS Open	17. REFERRED	18. TELETYPE NO.

CRIMINAL INVESTIGATION REPORT POLICE DEPARTMENT	1. General Broadcast? NO	2. COMPLAINT CONTROL NO. 05408176

3. TYPE OF REPORT Crime against person	4. INITIAL OR FOLLOW-UP Follow-Up (2)	5. COMPLAINT/ VICTIM'S NAME (Last, First, M.I.) MCFADDEN, Clyde P.
	6. PAGE 1 of 2	7. CRIME/ INCIDENT Shooting/Homicide

8. COMPLAINANT/WITNESS suspect Welch, Janie Ann	9. SEX /RACE F/W	10. LOCATION OF CRIME interior of private trailer

12. NARRATIVE: RECORD YOUR ACTIVITY AND ALL DEVELOPMENTS IN THIS CASE. INCLUDE ADDITIONAL VICTIMS WITNESSES AND SUSPECTS AS OUTLINED ABOVE. DESCRIBE DETAILS OF INCIDENT. DESCRIBE EVIDENCE AND PROPERTY AND INDICATE DISPOSITION:

WITNESSES:

1. Burns, Willie III: Employed in auto service department at Nellie's. Burns called the barrack reporting discovery of Clyde McFadden.

2. Wilson, George Lee Sr.: Employed at Soup Co. States he was with Janie Welch on the evening of murder between the hours of approximately 1900 hrs. and 2000 hrs. States that she left his home at that time (2000 hrs.) and returned at between 2025 and 2030 hrs., reporting McFadden's discovery. States that Janie is "quick tempered."

3. Lowes, Rufus: States that he was with Janie and Clyde on the morning of the murder. That there was no electronic equipment in the back of Clyde's van as stated by Janie. Advised that he telephoned the McFadden trailer on the evening of the murder at 1630 hrs. The phone rang but no answer. At 1800 to 1830 hrs. he telephoned the McFadden trailer and got a busy signal. Again, at 1845 and then at 2000 hrs. he telephoned the McFadden trailer. Each time he got a busy signal. He then got a friend of his to drive him to the McFadden trailer where he arrived between 2010 and 2015 hrs. The trailer lights, both interior and exterior, were on. Heard the television playing "real loud." The front door was locked. Knocked on door and window and got no answer. McFadden's van was not around.

15. INITIAL INVESTIGATOR I.D. NUMBER Linc Alton 0041	16. STATUS Open	17. REFERRED	18. TELETYPE NO.

CRIMINAL INVESTIGATION REPORT POLICE DEPARTMENT	1. General Broadcast? NO	2. COMPLAINT CONTROL NO. 05408176

3. TYPE OF REPORT Crime against person	4. INITIAL OR FOLLOW-UP Follow-Up (2)	5. COMPLAINT/ <u>VICTIM'S</u> NAME (Last, First, M.I.) MCFADDEN, Clyde P.
	6. PAGE 2 of 2	7. CRIME/ INCIDENT Shooting/Homicide

8. COMPLAINANT/WITNESS suspect Welch, Janie Ann	9. SEX /RACE F/W	10. LOCATION OF CRIME interior of private trailer

12. NARRATIVE: RECORD YOUR ACTIVITY AND ALL DEVELOPMENTS IN THIS CASE. INCLUDE ADDITIONAL VICTIMS WITNESSES AND SUSPECTS AS OUTLINED ABOVE. DESCRIBE DETAILS OF INCIDENT. DESCRIBE EVIDENCE AND PROPERTY AND INDICATE DISPOSITION:

WITNESSES:

4. Davis, Joe: Employed at soup company. Between 1130 hrs. and 1200 hrs. dropped off his moped bike at McFadden's trailer. He met Janie at trailer door. He returned at 1330 hrs. to pick up moped. At that time Janie was in the trailer.

5. Cranston, Loretta Ann: Employed at the chicken plant. States she sold a $10 bag of marijuana to Janie on the afternoon of the murder. During that sale, Janie told her that an old man had died and left her a mobile home, van and car. Stated she knew Janie was talking about Clyde McFadden because she knew Mr. McFadden and knew that he had a mobile home, a van, and a car.

6. Jones, Juanita: States that at around 1500 hours on afternoon of murder Janie told her an old man "got killed" and left her his stuff. Janie left her house shortly after arriving. Last saw Janie walking down the road away from Jones' house.

7. Banfield, Ann: employed at the community college. States that she has known Janie for more than four years. States that Janie began living with Clyde three or four weeks prior to murder. Describes Janie Welch as wild, a thief, a liar and vengeful.

8. Maxon, Delaine: Self-employed at Maxon Auto. States he loaned McFadden his .22 caliber auto-loading rifle the prior September in response to recent break-ins. Gun was fully loaded (fourteen bullets) at time of loan. Maxon did not give McFadden additional bullets. Owns the rifle used to shoot and beat Mr. McFadden to death.

15. INITIAL INVESTIGATOR I.D. NUMBER Linc Alton 0041	16. STATUS Open	17. REFERRED	18. TELETYPE NO.

CRIMINAL INVESTIGATION REPORT POLICE DEPARTMENT	1. General Broadcast? NO	2. COMPLAINT CONTROL NO. 05408176

3. TYPE OF REPORT Crime against person	4. INITIAL OR FOLLOW-UP Follow-Up (3)	5. COMPLAINT/ VICTIM'S NAME (Last, First, M.I.) MCFADDEN, Clyde P.
	6. PAGE 1 of 10	7. CRIME/ INCIDENT Shooting/Homicide

8. COMPLAINANT/WITNESS suspect Welch, Janie Ann	9. SEX /RACE F/W	10. LOCATION OF CRIME interior of private trailer

12. NARRATIVE: RECORD YOUR ACTIVITY AND ALL DEVELOPMENTS IN THIS CASE. INCLUDE ADDITIONAL VICTIMS WITNESSES AND SUSPECTS AS OUTLINED ABOVE. DESCRIBE DETAILS OF INCIDENT. DESCRIBE EVIDENCE AND PROPERTY AND INDICATE DISPOSITION:

On evening of murder, at approximately 2045 hrs., Willie Burns telephoned the barrack advising that there was an injured person at a trailer on West Road. Trooper Downing was directed to the trailer in question, later identified as residence of deceased (Clyde McFadden). Upon examination by Tpr. Downing, it was determined Mr. McFadden was deceased. The barrack was notified, whereupon I was directed to the scene. Upon arrival, at approximately 2130 hrs., I conducted a preliminary investigation.

McFadden was found lying on his stomach in front of his television on the living room floor. His arms were folded under his head. There was no evidence of one-on-one combat. It appeared Mr. McFadden was assailed from his rear, shot in back while he lay on the floor watching television. Examination of the body revealed the presence of at least five puncture wounds. Four giving the appearance of having been caused by four bullets, the fifth giving the appearance of having been caused by a knife. Further there was a gaping wound to the head which appeared to have been caused by many repeated blows. It appeared the assailant was acting in a rage - shooting, stabbing and bludgeoning the person of Clyde McFadden.

Found lying on the floor in the immediate vicinity of the body were six spent .22 caliber long rifle casings and four live .22 long rifle cartridges. In addition, two spent projectiles (.22 caliber bullets) were found. Further, a spring and metal

15. INITIAL INVESTIGATOR I.D. NUMBER Linc Alton 0041	16. STATUS Open	17. REFERRED	18. TELETYPE NO.

CRIMINAL INVESTIGATION REPORT POLICE DEPARTMENT		1. General Broadcast? NO	2. COMPLAINT CONTROL NO. 05408176
3. TYPE OF REPORT Crime against person	4. INITIAL OR FOLLOW-UP Follow-Up (3)	5. COMPLAINT/ VICTIM'S NAME (Last, First, M.I.) MCFADDEN, Clyde P.	
	6. PAGE 2 of 10	7. CRIME/ INCIDENT Shooting/Homicide	
8. COMPLAINANT/WITNESS suspect Welch, Janie Ann	9. SEX /RACE F/W	10. LOCATION OF CRIME interior of private trailer	

12. NARRATIVE: RECORD YOUR ACTIVITY AND ALL DEVELOPMENTS IN THIS CASE. INCLUDE ADDITIONAL VICTIMS WITNESSES AND SUSPECTS AS OUTLINED ABOVE. DESCRIBE DETAILS OF INCIDENT. DESCRIBE EVIDENCE AND PROPERTY AND INDICATE DISPOSITION:

plug which resembled the interior parts of a .22 caliber rifle were also found. The crime scene search revealed a broken .22 caliber, semi-automatic rifle behind a storage shed outside of and behind the rear of Mr. McFadden's trailer, the weapon was loaded with four live rounds. Also a large kitchen knife was found with the rifle. The initial examination of the knife revealed the presence of what appeared to be blood on the blade of the knife. There appeared to be hair, blood, and tissue on the broken rifle butt.

Further examination of the trailer revealed that the interior had been ransacked and that a rear, north-end bedroom window was broken by a brick having been thrown through it.

Janie Welch was at the crime scene and interviewed by me. Miss Welch advised that she was a live-in caretaker of Mr. McFadden's. Mr. McFadden was recovering from cancer and unable to totally care for himself. Miss Welch advised she did things such as cook Mr. McFadden's meals, clean the trailer, and run errands. Miss Welch advised the last time she saw Mr. McFadden alive was on the evening of the murder at 1730 hrs. It was at that time, according to Miss Welch, that she dropped McFadden off in front of his trailer, having been earlier picked up by him in his van out on Jersey Road. Miss Welch stated Mr. McFadden entered his trailer and locked the door, whereupon she padlocked an exterior door, got into Mr. McFadden's van, and drove away. Miss Welch advised she drove to the residence of her boyfriend,

15. INITIAL INVESTIGATOR I.D. NUMBER Linc Alton 0041	16. STATUS Open	17. REFERRED	18. TELETYPE NO.

CRIMINAL INVESTIGATION REPORT POLICE DEPARTMENT	1. General Broadcast? NO	2. COMPLAINT CONTROL NO. 05408176	

3. TYPE OF REPORT Crime against person	4. INITIAL OR FOLLOW-UP Follow-Up (3)	5. COMPLAINT/ VICTIM'S NAME (Last, First, M.I.) MCFADDEN, Clyde P.	
	6. PAGE 3 of 10	7. CRIME/ INCIDENT Shooting/Homicide	

8. COMPLAINANT/WITNESS suspect Welch, Janie Ann	9. SEX /RACE F/W	10. LOCATION OF CRIME interior of private trailer

12. NARRATIVE: RECORD YOUR ACTIVITY AND ALL DEVELOPMENTS IN THIS CASE. INCLUDE ADDITIONAL VICTIMS WITNESSES AND SUSPECTS AS OUTLINED ABOVE. DESCRIBE DETAILS OF INCIDENT. DESCRIBE EVIDENCE AND PROPERTY AND INDICATE DISPOSITION:

George Lee Wilson, Sr. According to Miss Welch, she stayed there until shortly before 2000 hours, when she left to return to the trailer in order to change her pants. Miss Welch advised she unlocked the trailer door, looked in and saw Mr. McFadden lying on the floor with blood about his head. Sensing that something was wrong, Miss Welch went back to Wilson's house in order to get assistance. Having told Wilson and two of his friends what she discovered, the four of them left Wilson's house and went to Mr. McFadden's trailer. Looking in the doorway, they observed Mr. McFadden on the floor, and left the scene without disturbing anything in order to telephone the police.

At the time of the initial interview with Miss Welch, she was very agitated, emotional, and nervous. Because of this, I decided to end my interview and re-interview her the following day. However, prior to her leaving, Miss Welch was asked if she could list any items that may have been stolen from the interior of the trailer. Miss Welch advised a small color television, vacuum cleaner, checkbook, and two bottles of prescription medicine (known to her as being Demerol) were missing.

Parked outside of the trailer was a 1998 van belonging to Mr. McFadden. The interior was examined whereupon a radio, a stereo amplifier, and a window fan were found. Janie Welch was asked what those items were doing in the van, whereupon she stated they "did not work" and that Mr. McFadden was going to "take them away to get rid of them."

15. INITIAL INVESTIGATOR I.D. NUMBER Linc Alton 0041	16. STATUS Open	17. REFERRED	18. TELETYPE NO.

CRIMINAL INVESTIGATION REPORT POLICE DEPARTMENT		1. General Broadcast? NO	2. COMPLAINT CONTROL NO. 05408176
3. TYPE OF REPORT Crime against person	4. INITIAL OR FOLLOW-UP Follow-Up (3)	5. COMPLAINT/ <u>VICTIM'S</u> NAME (Last, First, M.I.) MCFADDEN, Clyde P.	
	6. PAGE 4 of 10	7. CRIME/ INCIDENT Shooting/Homicide	
8. COMPLAINANT/WITNESS suspect Welch, Janie Ann	9. SEX /RACE F/W	10. LOCATION OF CRIME interior of private trailer	

12. NARRATIVE: RECORD YOUR ACTIVITY AND ALL DEVELOPMENTS IN THIS CASE. INCLUDE ADDITIONAL VICTIMS WITNESSES AND SUSPECTS AS OUTLINED ABOVE. DESCRIBE DETAILS OF INCIDENT. DESCRIBE EVIDENCE AND PROPERTY AND INDICATE DISPOSITION:

On the following day, a second interview was conducted and a typed and signed statement was obtained from Janie Welch at the police barracks. Miss Welch advised the following regarding her activities on the day of the murder:

She and Mr. McFadden awoke at approximately 0600 hours, drank a cup of coffee together, then left for the hospital so she could obtain her medicine (methadone). After receiving her medicine, Welch, McFadden, and a friend (Rufus Lowes) all went back to McFadden's trailer. Welch and McFadden later dropped Lowes off at his home around 0930 hours. They proceeded to the post office. From the post office, they drove to Hattie Notten's home where Miss Welch picked up her four-year-old son. From there, Welch advised, they went back to Mr. McFadden's trailer. It was about 1200 hrs. when they arrived. After about two hours, the three left Mr. McFadden's trailer to buy milk and drop Welch's son back at Notten's home.

Afterwards, Welch and McFadden returned to the trailer and Welch advised that a girlfriend (Juanita Jones) called and asked her to come over for a BBQ. At approximately 1500 hours, Miss Welch claims to have been picked up by a cab in front of Mr. McFadden's trailer and taken to the BBQ. At approximately 1730 hours, Miss Welch called Mr. McFadden from Juanita's house and asked him to come pick her up. Welch told McFadden to meet her on the main road because he didn't know where Juanita lived. Shortly thereafter, she was picked up by Mr. McFadden. They

15. INITIAL INVESTIGATOR I.D. NUMBER Linc Alton 0041	16. STATUS Open	17. REFERRED	18. TELETYPE NO.

	1. General Broadcast?	2. COMPLAINT CONTROL NO.
CRIMINAL INVESTIGATION REPORT POLICE DEPARTMENT	NO	05408176

3. TYPE OF REPORT	4. INITIAL OR FOLLOW-UP	5. COMPLAINT/ VICTIM'S NAME (Last, First, M.I.)
Crime against person	Follow-Up (3)	MCFADDEN, Clyde P.
	6. PAGE 5 of 10	7. CRIME/ INCIDENT Shooting/Homicide

8. COMPLAINANT/WITNESS suspect	9. SEX /RACE	10. LOCATION OF CRIME
Welch, Janie Ann	F/W	interior of private trailer

12. NARRATIVE: RECORD YOUR ACTIVITY AND ALL DEVELOPMENTS IN THIS CASE. INCLUDE ADDITIONAL VICTIMS WITNESSES AND SUSPECTS AS OUTLINED ABOVE. DESCRIBE DETAILS OF INCIDENT. DESCRIBE EVIDENCE AND PROPERTY AND INDICATE DISPOSITION:

went to get gas. At approximately 1800 hours, Miss Welch and Mr. McFadden arrived back at the trailer. Both exited the van. Mr. McFadden went into the trailer. Miss Welch padlocked the outside door, got into the van and drove off, driving to Wilson's house. There Miss Welch advised she talked with Wilson for over an hour. She left there and went for beer, then went back to McFadden's trailer to change her pants because it was getting cold. She unlocked the padlock, opened the front door, and saw blood on Mr. McFadden, whereupon she left and returned back to Wilson's house to inform him of her discovery.

Miss Welch was asked, "Have you ever seen a rifle in Clyde's home?" Her answer, "No, I never seen a rifle." Shortly after that question was asked, the interview was suspended for a break. Miss Welch was taken to the garage outside of the barrack and asked if she could identify the rifle and knife which had been found behind the shed late on the evening of the murder. Her reaction upon seeing the rifle was one of shock, her eyes opening wide, and she appeared to be stunned. Seeing her reaction, I knew that Janie had lied. I asked her about the rifle again. This time she advised that she had seen the rifle in Clyde's home before. She advised that she had seen the rifle in his bedroom on the day of the murder. Asked if she had ever used the rifle, she advised, "Yes, the last time was yesterday morning shooting at ducks." When asked why she denied the existence of the rifle, Janie stated the rifle was "hot,"

15. INITIAL INVESTIGATOR I.D. NUMBER	16. STATUS	17. REFERRED	18. TELETYPE NO.
Linc Alton 0041	Open		

		1. General Broadcast?	2. COMPLAINT CONTROL NO.
CRIMINAL INVESTIGATION REPORT **POLICE DEPARTMENT**		NO	05408176

3. TYPE OF REPORT	4. INITIAL OR FOLLOW-UP	5. COMPLAINT/ <u>VICTIM</u>'S NAME (Last, First, M.I.)
Crime against person	Follow-Up (3)	MCFADDEN, Clyde P.
	6. PAGE 6 of 10	7. CRIME/ INCIDENT Shooting/Homicide

8. COMPLAINANT/WITNESS suspect	9. SEX /RACE	10. LOCATION OF CRIME
Welch, Janie Ann	F/W	interior of private trailer

12. NARRATIVE: RECORD YOUR ACTIVITY AND ALL DEVELOPMENTS IN THIS CASE. INCLUDE ADDITIONAL VICTIMS WITNESSES AND SUSPECTS AS OUTLINED ABOVE. DESCRIBE DETAILS OF INCIDENT. DESCRIBE EVIDENCE AND PROPERTY AND INDICATE DISPOSITION:

because McFadden had bought the stolen weapon from a guy about a year earlier. Further she advised that having shot the rifle earlier in the day, she knew her fingerprints were on it.

Mr. Maxon, a longtime friend of Mr. McFadden's, advised that on the morning of the murder McFadden visited Maxon at his auto repair shop. Maxon saw Janie Welch in McFadden's van. Welch did not come into the shop. Part of the men's conversation centered on Welch.

Maxon advised that McFadden told him he (McFadden) was planning to evict Janie Welch from his home that weekend. At around 1100 hrs., Mr. McFadden left the auto shop. Mr. Maxon advised that he believed Janie Welch killed Clyde McFadden.

Two days after the murder, Miss Welch was interviewed a third time and taken to the area where she claimed to have fired the rifle on the morning of the murder. This area being directly across the road from Mr. McFadden's trailer. Miss Welch was asked to show where she shot the rifle so that the spent casings could be recovered. At this, Miss Welch became frustrated, agitated, and belligerent. She was stammering and unable to accurately point out where she had been shooting. It was evident from her behavior that Miss Welch did not know what to say. She pointed in several general directions which covered a wide area, saying that she shot the rifle "here and there." (A search of the area by me and Trooper Smith failed

15. INITIAL INVESTIGATOR I.D. NUMBER	16. STATUS	17. REFERRED	18. TELETYPE NO.
Linc Alton 0041	Open		

CRIMINAL INVESTIGATION REPORT POLICE DEPARTMENT		1. General Broadcast? NO	2. COMPLAINT CONTROL NO. 05408176
3. TYPE OF REPORT Crime against person	4. INITIAL OR FOLLOW-UP Follow-Up (3)	5. COMPLAINT/ VICTIM'S NAME (Last, First, M.I.) MCFADDEN, Clyde P.	
	6. PAGE 7 of 10	7. CRIME/ INCIDENT Shooting/Homicide	
8. COMPLAINANT/WITNESS suspect Welch, Janie Ann	9. SEX /RACE F/W	10. LOCATION OF CRIME interior of private trailer	

12. NARRATIVE: RECORD YOUR ACTIVITY AND ALL DEVELOPMENTS IN THIS CASE. INCLUDE ADDITIONAL VICTIMS WITNESSES AND SUSPECTS AS OUTLINED ABOVE. DESCRIBE DETAILS OF INCIDENT. DESCRIBE EVIDENCE AND PROPERTY AND INDICATE DISPOSITION:

to reveal the existence of any spent .22 caliber long rifle casings).

Four days after the murder George Wilson (Janie Welch's boyfriend) was interviewed. Mr. Wilson advised that he had known Janie Welch for some time. He describes her as being "quick tempered" among other things. He advised that Janie Welch arrived at his home at approximately 1900 hours. Then she left at approximately 2000 hours and returned a second time, reporting the discovery of Mr. McFadden between 2025 and 2030 hours. He stated that Tony Strom was at his home when Janie arrived the first time, and that Willie Burns arrived shortly after Janie departed and that it was dark when Willie arrived.

Five days after the murder, Janie Welch was interviewed a fourth time. On this occasion she was advised of her Miranda rights, whereupon she signed a written waiver. On this occasion, Miss Welch was asked how she fired the rifle on the morning of the murder when she went "duck shooting." She said she had to function each shot. She had to pull a lever to make a bullet pop out, and another go in. During this interview, Miss Welch advised that after shooting the rifle she went back to McFadden's trailer and placed the rifle behind a curtain in the living room. She advised that Mr. McFadden saw the rifle behind the curtain, took it to his bedroom, whereupon he reloaded the rifle. (It should be noted that a thorough examination of the interior and exterior of the crime scene failed to reveal

15. INITIAL INVESTIGATOR I.D. NUMBER Linc Alton 0041	16. STATUS Open	17. REFERRED	18. TELETYPE NO.

CRIMINAL INVESTIGATION REPORT POLICE DEPARTMENT		1. General Broadcast? NO	2. COMPLAINT CONTROL NO. 05408176
3. TYPE OF REPORT Crime against person	4. INITIAL OR FOLLOW-UP Follow-Up (3)	5. COMPLAINT/ VICTIM'S NAME (Last, First, M.I.) MCFADDEN, Clyde P.	
	6. PAGE 8 of 10	7. CRIME/ INCIDENT Shooting/Homicide	
8. COMPLAINANT/WITNESS-suspect Welch, Janie Ann	9. SEX /RACE F/W	10. LOCATION OF CRIME interior of private trailer	

12. NARRATIVE: RECORD YOUR ACTIVITY AND ALL DEVELOPMENTS IN THIS CASE. INCLUDE ADDITIONAL VICTIMS WITNESSES AND SUSPECTS AS OUTLINED ABOVE. DESCRIBE DETAILS OF INCIDENT. DESCRIBE EVIDENCE AND PROPERTY AND INDICATE DISPOSITION:

the presence of any .22 caliber ammunition other than what has already been mentioned. There was no empty, full, or partially full box of .22 ammunition in Mr. McFadden's trailer or garbage.)

Miss Welch was advised that the electronic equipment previously mentioned, which had been found in Mr. McFadden's van, had been tested and found to be completely operable. With this, Miss Welch advised that she took the items out of the house and put them in the van because she was in the process of moving that day. She advised that Mr. McFadden did not want her to go, so she stopped taking the items. She advised that Mr. McFadden wanted her to stay the winter with him. Miss Welch advised that Mr. McFadden was giving her the aforementioned items to use in her new home. When questioned as to the location of her new home, it was observed that Miss Welch fumbled with an answer, became frustrated and agitated, and was unable to provide any type of answer other than to say she was looking for a new home. When confronted with her previous statement about the items being inoperable, she advised she did not make that statement, and repeated that McFadden gave her the items.

When asked about Mr. McFadden's drugs, specifically the Demerol, Miss Welch advised that she had taken some for herself, that she had sold some to a friend, and that she had left a few pills in the vial for Mr. McFadden to see.

Six days after the murder, Juanita Jones was interviewed. Juanita advised that she did not have a BBQ on the afternoon

15. INITIAL INVESTIGATOR I.D. NUMBER Linc Alton 0041	16. STATUS Open	17. REFERRED	18. TELETYPE NO.

CRIMINAL INVESTIGATION REPORT POLICE DEPARTMENT		1. General Broadcast? NO	2. COMPLAINT CONTROL NO. 05408176
3. TYPE OF REPORT Crime against person	4. INITIAL OR FOLLOW-UP Follow-Up (3)	5. COMPLAINT/ <u>VICTIM</u>'S NAME (Last, First, M.I.) MCFADDEN, Clyde P.	
	6. PAGE 9 of 10	7. CRIME/ INCIDENT Shooting/Homicide	
8. COMPLAINANT/WITNESS s̶u̶s̶p̶e̶c̶t̶ Welch, Janie Ann	9. SEX /RACE F/W	10. LOCATION OF CRIME interior of private trailer	

12. NARRATIVE: RECORD YOUR ACTIVITY AND ALL DEVELOPMENTS IN THIS CASE. INCLUDE ADDITIONAL VICTIMS WITNESSES AND SUSPECTS AS OUTLINED ABOVE. DESCRIBE DETAILS OF INCIDENT. DESCRIBE EVIDENCE AND PROPERTY AND INDICATE DISPOSITION:

of the murder, and that she did not call and invite Janie Welch to a BBQ. She stated that Janie Welch arrived unannounced at approximately 1500 hours on the day of the murder. Janie told Juanita that "a middle age guy had got killed and left her his trailer, van and car." Juanita advised that she did not believe Janie's statement because she feels that no one would leave anything to Janie Welch. Welch left shortly after arriving.

As is evident from the facts reported above, Janie Welch knew of the demise or future demise of Clyde McFadden at least five hours prior to her report of his death at George Wilson's house. Further, it is evident there is considerable discrepancy between Welch and Wilson as to when Janie Welch initially arrived at his house and the time given by Juanita Jones as to when Janie left her home. Clyde McFadden died as a result of being shot by a person who was able to be in the same room with him without causing any apprehension on his part. Items that were initially reported stolen by Miss Welch (a small color television, checkbook, and prescribed drugs) were in fact not stolen. A canvassing of witnesses indicates that Mr. McFadden did not own a small color television. Miss Welch later admitted taking the Demerol. And, to this date, no checks have been uttered on McFadden's account.

Miss Welch initially denied the existence of a .22 caliber rifle. When confronted with its discovery, she admitted lying about it and said she lied about it because it was stolen and

15. INITIAL INVESTIGATOR I.D. NUMBER Linc Alton 0041	16. STATUS Open	17. REFERRED	18. TELETYPE NO.

		1. General Broadcast?	2. COMPLAINT CONTROL NO.
CRIMINAL INVESTIGATION REPORT POLICE DEPARTMENT		NO	05408176

3. TYPE OF REPORT	4. INITIAL OR FOLLOW-UP	5. COMPLAINT/ <u>VICTIM'S</u> NAME (Last, First, M.I.)
Crime against person	Follow-Up (3)	MCFADDEN, Clyde P.

	6. PAGE	7. CRIME/ INCIDENT
	10 of 10	Shooting/Homicide

8. COMPLAINANT/WITNESS ~~suspect~~	9. SEX /RACE	10. LOCATION OF CRIME
Welch, Janie Ann	F/W	interior of private trailer

12. NARRATIVE: RECORD YOUR ACTIVITY AND ALL DEVELOPMENTS IN THIS CASE. INCLUDE ADDITIONAL VICTIMS WITNESSES AND SUSPECTS AS OUTLINED ABOVE. DESCRIBE DETAILS OF INCIDENT. DESCRIBE EVIDENCE AND PROPERTY AND INDICATE DISPOSITION:

because her fingerprints were on it. In fact, the gun was not stolen, it was on loan to Mr. McFadden from Mr. Maxon, and further it was felt that she did not fire the weapon as she claims because to have done so would have resulted in there being fewer bullets in the rifle than the "fully-loaded" fourteen (all of which were accounted for either in the weapon, or in spent casings around Mr. McFadden's body).

From interviews, it was learned that on the afternoon of the murder Janie Welch had been smoking marijuana, drinking malt liquor, and as is now known, had received methadone at 0900 hours that day.

Based on information, fact, and circumstances reported herein, the following is concluded: Clyde McFadden met his death at the hands of Janie Welch who was acting in "rage" having been told of her imminent eviction. After his demise, she staged a break-in, reporting items stolen that were in fact not stolen.

Upon receipt of additional information, another supplemental report will be submitted. Until such time, it is requested that this report be closed by the arrest of Janie Welch.

15. INITIAL INVESTIGATOR I.D. NUMBER	16. STATUS	17. REFERRED	18. TELETYPE NO.
Linc Alton 0041	Open		

Points to Consider:

1. **Making the Initial Contact:** You will be meeting with the client for the first time in the local jail. What steps if any will you take to ensure the confidentiality of the meeting? In addition, you are a relatively inexperienced law student. Your client is facing very serious charges. What steps will you take to persuade the client she is in good hands? Finally, you may be asking the client about sensitive topics (including her inconsistent statements to the police, her seeming awareness of the murder before she finally reported it, and her drug use) what will you do to broach these topics in a way that helps to ensure candor and completeness? On the other hand, do you want complete candor from your client? If not, why not?

2. **Framing the Conversation:** Your supervising attorney has asked you to gather information to 1) help identify an investigatory strategy, 2) make some preliminary assessments related to the defense strategy, and 3) at least begin to consider the advisability of a plea. Will you be candid with the client about all of these goals? If not, why not? If so, why?

3. **Confronting Bias:** The initial police reports suggest that the victim met a horrifically violent death, and your client, at least initially, appears to be the most likely suspect. On the other hand, there is a significant age difference between the victim and the client and you are aware of some potential vulnerabilities your client possesses (she is a single mother with a drug problem whose child appears to be in the custody of another person), which may raise questions about the nature of her relationship with the victim. Are you aware of any personal biases you hold that will make it difficult for you to approach this interview with an open mind? If so, what will you do to accomplish your professional goals in spite of them?

CHAPTER 3

Fast Car

Drafting a Client Letter

YOU ARE WORKING AS an intern at the Appellate Project, a Maryland non-profit that handles criminal appeals for indigent defendants. During your time in the office, you represented a client who was convicted of theft charges. Earlier this morning you received the appellate court's decision reversing your client's conviction. You must now draft a letter to the client informing her of the news. In connection with that task, you have the following documents: 1) an assignment memo from your supervisor, 2) the appellate court opinion, and 3) the contact card for the client.

Memorandum

To: You
From: Supervisor
Re: Congrats, you won!

Thanks again for your hard work on the James case. We just received a copy of the decision. You won! The court has reversed James' conviction and remanded the case for further proceedings in the lower court.

As you know because this is an appellate office, we do not handle the client's case on remand. We will instead hand the case off to the public defender's office for any further proceedings. Please draft a letter to the client informing her of the court's decision and closing out the representation.

Your letter should give James a brief and straightforward explanation of the court's reasoning. You should also make clear to James that our representation is coming to a close, but that her case will be handed off to another attorney at the public defender's office.

I know you met with James at the beginning of the representation before we filed our briefs and before the argument. After sending your letter, please also make plans to go out to see James in the next two weeks so that you can close out the representation in person, and answer any questions she may have about the decision or next steps.

Run the letter by me before sending it out. Thx!

UNREPORTED

IN THE COURT OF APPEALS
No. 2191
September Term

JESSICA JAMES

v.

STATE

Ellis, H.L.,
Middleton, M.S.B.,
Latimer, S.T. (Specially Assigned),
JJ.

Opinion by Latimer, S.T.

Appellant, Jessica James, was tried before a jury in the Circuit Court on seven counts: (1) first degree burglary; (2) third degree burglary; (3) fourth degree burglary; (4 & 5) two counts of theft over $500; (6) theft less than $500; and (7) malicious destruction of property with a value of less than $500. At the pre-trial motions hearing, appellant moved to suppress evidence seized during a warrantless search of her car. That motion was denied. Prior to trial, the court also denied appellant's request for a continuance, which she sought in order to locate Julius Inmark, a witness for the defense.

Following the close of evidence, the jury acquitted appellant of all three counts of burglary (Counts 1-3), one count of theft over $500 (Count 4), and malicious destruction of property (Count 7). The trial court granted a motion for judgment of acquittal on the second count for theft over $500 (Count 5). The jury convicted appellant on two counts of theft less than $500—the lesser included offense for Count 4 and the offense charged in Count 6. After denying defense counsel's request to suspend the sentence, the court sentenced appellant to two years in prison. This appeal followed.

Questions Presented

Appellant presents the following questions:

1. Is reversal required where the trial court refused to suppress evidence seized during a warrantless search of Jessica James' car, though officers did not conduct the search incident to Jessica James' arrest until after she was secured in the back seat of a patrol car?

2. Did the trial court abuse its discretion when it failed to grant the defense request for a brief continuance, where the continuance was requested so that counsel could obtain a necessary witness who would have assumed complete responsibility for the stolen items that were found during a warrantless search of the backseat and trunk of Jessica James' "loaner" car?

We answer the first question in the affirmative and reverse appellant's convictions. As such, we need not address the second question.

Facts

At the hearing on appellant's motion to suppress, defense counsel stated that the issue before the court was that "there was no probable cause for the arrest at the time the arrest was made" and, therefore, everything seized from appellant's person and car, and all statements made, should be suppressed. In response to the motion, the State called Officer Corey Nolan of the Howard County Police Department. Nolan testified that while driving eastbound on Hickory Ridge Road, he observed a tan Nissan vehicle with no front tag and a cracked front windshield. As the vehicle passed, Nolan "saw the rear tag and [ ] conducted an MVA check." After making a U-turn, Nolan was informed by the National Crime Information Center that the tag was stolen.

Nolan testified that "[t]he vehicle had turned in 10760 Hickory Ridge Road and had parked in a parking spot," next to a convenience store. Appellant then stepped out of the vehicle and "was walking away from the vehicle when [Nolan] made contact with her." Appellant allowed Nolan to "pat her down very quickly for weapons just to make sure everything was safe." Nolan asked for identification but appellant said "she did not have her ID on her." Appellant, however, told Nolan that her name was "Jessie James."

When asked about the stolen tag, appellant informed Nolan that "the car did belong her, [but] she didn't know the tag was stolen." Nolan then ran the Nissan's Vehicle Information Number through dispatch and discovered that the car was not registered to appellant. Once again, Nolan "ran the tag through dispatch," and was informed that "the tag was listed . . . to a Mercury vehicle." Upon confirming that "the tag was, in fact, stolen," Nolan advised appellant that she was under arrest for theft. Thereafter, Nolan searched appellant's person, and appellant was secured in Nolan's patrol car pursuant to her arrest for the stolen tag. After the appellant was placed under arrest, her car was "ultimately" searched.

The searches yielded several items which, together with subsequent statements made by appellant, linked appellant to a recent residential burglary, and became the subject of the motion to suppress. Appellant was "ultimately transported to the Howard County Detention Center."

After hearing argument from the State and defense counsel, the court denied appellant's motion to suppress with respect to the physical evidence, and granted it with respect to the statements. The court then asked whether counsel understood the ruling. Defense counsel answered in the affirmative. The hearing concluded immediately thereafter.

Discussion

Appellant argues that the trial court erred when it denied her motion to suppress because, "among other things, police officers did not conduct the search until after [she] was arrested and detained in the backseat of a patrol car." In its brief, the State responds by stating that: (1) this argument is not preserved; (2) even if preserved, the police had probable cause to search appellant's vehicle; and (3) the vehicle's contents inevitably would have been discovered in a subsequent inventory search. In light of the Supreme Court's imposition of substantial limits on the warrantless search of vehicles following arrest of the occupants, *Arizona v. Gant*, 129 S. Ct. 1710, 1714 (2009), we hold that the circuit court erred in denying appellant's motion to suppress.

Standard of Review

In reviewing the denial of a motion to suppress evidence, "we look only to the record of the suppression hearing and do not consider any evidence adduced at trial." *Daniels v. State*, 172 Md. App. 75, 87 (2006). "[W]e extend great deference to the fact finding of the suppression court and accept the facts as found by that court unless clearly erroneous." *Crosby v. State*, 408 Md. 490, 504-05 (2009). Further, we view the evidence "in the light most favorable to the party that prevailed on the motion," the State. *Id.* at 504. Nevertheless, in determining whether there was a Fourth Amendment violation, "we 'make our own independent constitutional appraisal by reviewing the law and applying it to the facts of the case.'" *Id.* at 505 (quoting *State v. Williams*, 401 Md. 676, 678 (2007)).

Preservation

The State argues that appellant's claim regarding the suppression of evidence is not preserved because, "at the suppression hearing below, James did not present the argument now offered on appeal." Specifically, the State points out that, during the hearing, appellant "focused her motion to suppress evidence exclusively on her claim that there was no probable cause for her arrest." Meanwhile, on appeal, appellant contends that the vehicle search conducted incident to her arrest was unconstitutional.

Maryland Rule 8-131(a) provides that, "[o]rdinarily, the appellate court will not decide any other issue unless it plainly appears by the record to have been raised in or decided by the trial court." Thus, an appellate court can rule on a decision based on a ground not raised below "only when it is clear that it will not work an unfair prejudice to the parties or to the court." *State v. Bell*, 334 Md. 178, 189 (1994).

The State argues in its brief that, during the suppression hearing, defense counsel argued at trial that everything seized from appellant's person and car, and all statements made, should be suppressed because "there was no probable cause for the arrest at the time the arrest was made." The State's argument is flawed, however, because after hearing testimony and argument, the court ruled that the arrest was proper and, in so doing, ultimately decided the issue of suppression of the items found in the vehicle appellant was driving. *See* Md. Rule 8-131(a), *supra*.

In this case, all of the evidence and the ruling of the court addressed the issue of suppression. By ruling on the legality of the arrest, the court necessarily had to decide whether the evidence seized from appellant's person and vehicle which she was driving should be suppressed. As such, the issue has been preserved for our review.

Arizona v. Gant

Turning to the merits, we discuss the application of *Gant* to this case. For decades, the Supreme Court has embraced the general rule that searches conducted without a warrant are "per se unreasonable" and thereby violate the Fourth Amendment to the United States Constitution. *See, e.g., Katz v. United States*, 389 U.S. 347, 357 (1967). "The point of the Fourth Amendment, which often is not grasped by zealous officers, is not that it denies law enforcement the support of the usual inferences which reasonable men draw from evidence." *Johnson v. United States*, 333 U.S. 10, 13-14 (1948). Rather, it requires "that those inferences be drawn by a neutral and detached magistrate instead of being judged by the officer engaged in the often competitive enterprise of ferreting out crime." *Id.* at 14; *see also United States v. Lefkowitz*, 285 U.S. 452, 464 (1932) ("Security against unlawful searches is more likely to be attained by resort to search warrants than by reliance upon the caution and sagacity of petty officers while acting under the excitement that attends the capture of persons accused of crime.").

In keeping with its recognition of the overwhelming preference for warrants, the Supreme Court has been careful to carve out only a handful of "specifically established and well-delineated exceptions" to the warrant requirement. Katz, *supra*, 389 U.S. at 357. For example, the presence of exigent circumstances, such as the hot pursuit of a fleeing felon, will excuse a warrantless search. *Warden, Md. Penitentiary v. Hayden*, 387 U.S. 294, 298 (1967). Similarly, the warrantless stop and frisk of an individual for the limited purposes of briefly investigating reasonably suspicious behavior and ensuring officer safety are permissible. *Terry v. Ohio*, 392 U.S. 1, 27 (1968). Exceptions to the warrant requirement have also been carved out for: consent searches, *Schneckloth v. Bustamonte*, 412 U.S. 218, 248-49 (1973); items in plain view, *Coolidge v. N.H.*, 403 U.S. 443, 465 (1971); searches in heavily regulated industries, *N.Y. v. Burger*, 482 U.S. 691, 707-09 (1987); "special needs" searches, *Vernonia Sch. Dist. 47j v. Acton*, 515 U.S. 646, 653 (1995); and searches of automobiles where the officer has probable cause for believing that the vehicle is "carrying contraband or illegal merchandise," *Carroll v. United States*, 267 U.S. 132, 149, 154 (1925).

Of particular relevance to the present case is the Supreme Court's decision in *Chimel v. California*, 395 U.S. 752, 762-63 (1969), where it held that warrantless searches may be conducted incident to a valid arrest. The *Chimel* Court limited such searches, however, to "the arrestee's person and the area within his immediate control." *Id.* at 763. Twelve years later, in *New York v. Belton*, 453 U.S. 454, 460 (1981), the Supreme Court extended the *Chimel* rule to allow a search of the entire interior of a car immediately following the arrest of its occupants.

In 2009, the Supreme Court decided *Gant* and rejected a broad interpretation of *Belton*, holding that "*Belton* does not authorize a vehicle search incident to a recent occupant's arrest after the arrestee has been secured and cannot access the interior of the vehicle." *Gant, supra*, 129 S. Ct. at 1714. The *Gant* Court added, however, that "circumstances unique to the automobile context justify a search incident to arrest when it is reasonable to believe that evidence of the offense of arrest might be found in the vehicle." *Id.*

In *Gant*, police officers received an anonymous tip that a particular residence in Tucson, Arizona, was "being used to sell drugs." *Id.* The officers "knocked on the front door and asked to speak to the owner." *Id.* "Gant answered the door and, after identifying himself, stated that he expected the owner to return later." *Id.* at 1714-15. Subsequently, the officers "conducted a records check, which revealed that Gant's driver's license had been suspended and there was an outstanding warrant for his arrest for driving with a suspended license." *Id.* at 1715. The officers returned to the home that evening, at which time they observed Gant pull into the driveway. *Id.* After Gant exited the car, one of the officers "immediately arrested Gant and handcuffed him." *Id.* "When two more officers arrived, they locked Gant in the backseat of their vehicle." *Id.* Thereafter, "two officers searched his car: One of them found a gun, and the other discovered a bag of cocaine in the pocket of a jacket on the backseat." *Id.* Gant was charged. Prior to trial, he moved to suppress the evidence seized from his car. *Id.*

Upon review, the Supreme Court held that the exception to the warrant requirement recognized in *Belton* did not justify the warrantless search of Gant's car. *Id.* at 1719. Specifically, the *Gant* Court noted that the exception recognized in *Belton* was derived from "interests in officer safety and evidence preservation that are typically implicated in arrest situations." *Id.* at 1716. Thus, police officers are authorized "to search a vehicle incident to a recent occupant's arrest only when the arrestee is unsecured and within reaching distance of the passenger compartment at the time of the search." *Id.* at 1719. Because Gant was secured in the backseat of a patrol car when officers initiated the search, there was "no possibility that [he] could reach into the area that law enforcement officers [sought] to search" and, therefore, the warrantless search was not authorized. *Id.* at 1716.

In addition to the arrestee's access to the car, the *Gant* Court noted that the search incident to arrest doctrine might, in a narrow range of circumstances, justify the search of a car to locate evidence. *Id.* at 1719. Such a search would be appropriate "when it is 'reasonable to believe evidence relevant to the crime of arrest might be found in the vehicle.'" *Id.* (quoting *Thornton v. United States*, 541 U.S. 615, 632 (2004) (Scalia, J., concurring in judgment)). According to the *Gant* Court, "[i]n many cases, as when a recent occupant is arrested for a traffic violation, there will be no reasonable basis to believe the vehicle contains relevant evidence." *Id.* In contrast, where there is a drug or gun charge, "the offense of arrest will supply a basis for searching the passenger compartment of an arrestee's vehicle and any containers therein." *Id.*

In this case, Officer Nolan initially stopped appellant because her car had a cracked windshield, was missing a front tag, and an inquiry revealed that the rear tag was stolen.

After frisking appellant for weapons, Officer Nolan confirmed that the rear tag was stolen, and subsequently placed appellant under arrest for theft. While appellant was secured in a patrol car, officers searched her vehicle.

Based upon this record, the court's denial of appellant's motion to suppress was erroneous. Here, as in *Gant*, "[n]either the possibility of access nor the likelihood of discovering offense-related evidence authorized the search." *Id*. At the time her vehicle was searched, appellant was secured, far from being within reaching distance of her car. Moreover, appellant's arrest for a stolen tag did not give probable cause to believe that additional evidence of the offense for which she was arrested would be found in her vehicle. Therefore, any evidence yielded by the search should have been suppressed, and appellant's convictions now warrant reversal.

Probable Cause

The State argues that the court acted properly in denying appellant's motion to suppress because "probable cause existed to search the vehicle for a second stolen plate, for the tools or instruments used to perpetrate the theft, or for registration or identification documents relating to the vehicle, or even for the proper tags for the vehicle." Nothing in the record, however, suggests that the police officers were looking for these specific items during their search. In addition, the State had the opportunity to, but did not, present any testimony to support the likelihood of finding such items in a person's vehicle, after that person is arrested for theft of a license plate. To the contrary, it can be inferred that possession of a rear license plate alone provides enough evidence to support a charge of theft of a license plate. Thus, the State's argument fails.

Inevitable Discovery

Finally, the State argues that the court properly denied appellant's motion to suppress because "the evidence found in the vehicle would inevitably have been discovered during a subsequent inventory search." In making this argument, the

State "presumes" that, following James' arrest, the police "impounded the vehicle with the stolen tag." Thus, relying on *Gibson v. State*, 138 Md. App 399 (2001), the State contends that the evidence was properly received because it "'ultimately or inevitably would have been discovered.'" *Id.* at 404 (quoting *Nix v. Williams*, 467 U.S. 431, 444 (1984)).

We agree with appellant that the doctrine of inevitable discovery is inapplicable, as there is no evidence to support the State's claim that, after appellant's arrest, the vehicle was - or would have been - impounded and searched. In fact, nowhere in the transcript of the suppression hearing does it state that the car was towed, impounded, or transferred to a holding facility, as per police protocol. In addition, there was no testimony presented regarding the standard procedures for inventory searches of cars, or a description of which cars, in particular, would be subject to an inventory search. Therefore, we reject the State's contention that "[t]he items seized from James' vehicle were . . . admissible under the inevitable discovery rule."

For all of the foregoing reasons, we reverse appellant's convictions.

JUDGMENTS OF THE CIRCUIT COURT REVERSED. COSTS TO BE PAID BY THE COUNTY

Client **Contact Card**

Jessica James
Inmate Id. No. 324-298

Western Correctional Institution for Women
P.O. Box 124
Anytown, Here 12345

Authorized family contacts:

Gloria (mother)
Jesse (brother)

CHAPTER 4

The Children's Crusade

Retainer Letter and Suppression Strategy Outline

YOU ARE WORKING AS a new associate at a well-respected, mid-sized law firm in the city. Though the firm primarily handles plaintiff-side complex civil litigation, it also takes on a fair number of high profile criminal matters. After taking reputational hits on a couple of really tough criminal cases, the firm has become more cautious and selective when taking on new matters.

Earlier this morning, you received a call in the office from an old high school classmate, Summer Rose. After exchanging pleasantries, Rose explains that she is calling because she is being prosecuted and needs a lawyer. She has heard really good things about your firm and is hoping you will take the case. Intrigued (and delirious at the prospect of bringing in new business so soon) you ask her to tell you more. You have the following conversation:

> **YOU:** *So, tell me a little bit more about what happened.*

> **S.R.:** *Well, after high school, I fell on some hard times. I picked up a pretty bad heroin habit, and started running with a pretty tough crowd. When I got in too deep with my dealer, he said he'd clear my accounts if I did him a favor.*

> **YOU:** *Well, so far, it doesn't sound like you're in much need of a lawyer. A bodyguard maybe ... but I'm not hearing much of a criminal case yet.*

S.R.: *Let me finish . . . I'm getting to that. But, before I get to the details. I can talk to you right? I mean, I know we go way back, but this is serious and I need your word that you're not going to tell anyone what I'm about to tell you.*

YOU: *You've got my word; this is just between us.*

S.R.: *Okay, here's the deal. My dealer is a pretty tough dude. He runs heroin and coke. But, his real money is in people. He brings young kids in from all over the world. He's got this huge warehouse over on Barrow Street where he holds them until they can be sold. Anyway, he asked me to work as one of the kind of like babysitters, you know. There were five of us. We were responsible for all of the kids. We stayed at the warehouse and made sure everyone shared the food and didn't fight and didn't try to leave. We also made sure the kids kept the place clean and didn't make a lot of noise. Some of the other babysitters got paid, but I was just working down my debt. I was only there for a couple of days.*

YOU: *Holy cow . . . you're involved in that case?! It's been all over the news. You know those kids were being sold to drug gangs! They were being used as runners and street soldiers and stuff. What were you thinking?*

S.R.: *I wasn't really. I was just doing a friend a favor and working down my debt. A win-win. I didn't ask where the kids were going. For all I knew it was like an adoption agency or something. You know . . . giving them a better life.*

YOU: *They were holding something like twenty kids in there!!! And, one of the news reports said the warehouse was padlocked from the outside. Was that true? Where you locked in there?*

S.R.: *Yeah, there were four doors and they were all padlocked. The windows had bars installed on the inside—stupid me . . . what's that saying . . . "the jailer is in jail too." Really though, it wasn't so bad, the dealer sent his guys by everyday to drop off food and supplies. Sometimes they'd pick up kids, other times they'd drop new kids off. All of us babysitters stayed down on the first floor and it was a pretty nice set up—I mean, we had cable and a bathroom with a shower, and a table where we could eat and play cards and stuff. The folks I was working with were pretty decent, with the exception of this one dude . . . gosh, what a crack head! The kids were all up on the second floor. They had mattresses lined up around the walls and there was a bathroom with a couple of toilets and sinks. And, like I said, we made them keep it clean. We weren't monsters or anything. We were pretty nice to them. They had to be handcuffed to each other in groups of three. But, we mostly left them alone if they were doing what they were supposed to do. Almost none of them spoke any English, so it wasn't like we were going to be best buddies. Anyway, as you saw on the news, the police raided the place last week, and found the guns the dealer gave us and the cell phones and stuff. They also found a bunch of paperwork we kept on the kids. Those bastards have charged me and the other babysitters with a bunch of stuff. I was lucky I posted bond. The bail judge was pretty angry, but I told her I was just as much a prisoner as those kids were! Please tell me you can help me.*

YOU: *If you were locked in there too, we'll be able to get you off. We had another case a lot like this and we won there. But, hang tight, don't talk to anyone and I'll be in touch in a day or so.*

S.R.: *Okay, you can reach me on my cell . . . that's this number. You can also reach me by email at Summer@Rose.com; or at my dad's house 1234 Homeplace Street, Anytown, State, 54321. He's allowing me to crash there until this thing blows over.*

After hanging up the phone, you go online and pull up news stories about the raid. You learn that the local cable company contacted the police after it was asked to set up a new customer account in what the company believed was an empty warehouse. Suspecting possible theft of cable services, a cable company employee visited the location several months after the installation to look for pirated cable lines running from the warehouse to other nearby structures. Unable to see any, the cable employee walked up and down the sidewalk in front of the building. He thought he heard noise coming from inside, but saw padlocks on the only two doors on the front of the building. Convinced that some sort of cable fraud was taking place, the employee left and reported his findings to his supervisors, who contacted the police.

A day or two after the cable guy's visit, Officers Jim Mallon and Daisy Fortas drove out to the warehouse. The police officers saw the pad-locks on the two front doors. They walked around to the back of the building and found padlocks on the two rear doors as well. There was also a locked roll-down metal grate over what appeared to be a small loading dock on the side of the building. As the officers were walking around the outside of the building, the cable company called and reported that a streaming movie service was currently being used at the location. Officers Mallon and Fortas walked across the street and (with the homeowner's permission) climbed onto the stoop of a row house. From this vantage point, the officers were able to see a second story to the warehouse that was located on the back half of the build-ing. The officers could see an open window with fluttering curtains, but couldn't see inside. They called for backup.

When backup arrived, Fortas, Mallon and a third officer placed a ladder against the warehouse and climbed onto the roof of the loading dock. They walked across the roof and looked into the second story window. They saw metal bars on the inside of the window. They also saw young children huddled together around the edges of a large room. The children appeared to be chained to each other in small groups. The kids, who looked undernourished and scared, did not communicate with the officers. Believing the situation presented a public safety emergency, the officers cut the padlocks off the doors.

Inside, the officers found twenty-three children between the ages of ten and seventeen. The police also found five adults (including Summer Rose) all in their early twenties. The adults were immediately placed under arrest, but were not read their rights or immediately transferred to the police station. The children were separated for questioning. Agents from Immigration and Customs Enforcement were called to the scene and quickly determined that the adults were U.S. citizens, but the children were in the country illegally.

As the ICE agents were working with the children, Mallon and Fortas walked around the first floor of the warehouse to ensure no one else was being held in the warehouse. As they looked for other children, the officers also moved things, picked things up, and examined them. As he walked, Officer Mallon saw paperwork scattered across a table. He immediately recognized the paperwork as records of human trafficking. Mallon also saw rags stuffed into a large hole in the wall behind the table. He removed the rags, reached into the hole, and retrieved three loaded handguns. On the table, the officer also saw ammunition, a Taser, and a book titled, "Keeping Kids Quiet: Ten Methods to Effectively Control Children Without Violence."

You meet with the partners in the firm's New Business Group, they agree the case is interesting, but several of the more cautious part-ners want to hedge their bets before taking on the full representation. They ask you to draft a retainer that limits the scope of representation to pre-trial matters only. If at least some of the evidence cannot be suppressed/excluded, they want you to inform the client that the representation will end. The partners also want you to prepare a flowchart or outline of a rough strategy for suppression/exclusion. Your flowchart/outline should identify (1) each piece of evidence you believe can possibly be kept out, (2) the constitutional principles that support suppression/exclusion, and (3) the argument(s) you anticipate the government will make to defeat your motions.

 ## Points to Consider:

1. **Making Contact:** The partners have asked you to draft a retainer, and you have assured the client you will "be in touch" in a couple of days. Once you have determined what you are going to say, your next decision will be how to communicate that message to the client. You have a telephone number, an e-mail address and a mailing address. There are relative up-sides and down-sides to each of these methods of communication. Which will you use?

2. **Limiting the Retainer:** The partners have asked you to confine the scope of representation to pre-trial suppression matters. Only if you are successful pre-trial will you continue to work with the client. Do you have any concerns about limiting the representation in this fashion? Do you think such a limitation is enforceable?

3. **Sources of Law:** In thinking about the likelihood of suppression/exclusion, there are a number of provisions that protect people like Summer Rose. You have learned about four primary sources of constitutional protection for criminal defendants—the Fourth, Fifth, Sixth and Eighth Amendments. Which of those constitutional protections are implicated by the facts of the instant case?

4. **The Katz Test:** As you have learned, not everyone is protected by the Fourth Amendment. Instead, only those with a reasonable expectation of privacy may assert a Fourth Amendment violation. Do you have any concerns about Summer Rose's ability to establish a reasonable expectation of privacy in the instant case?

CHAPTER 5

Hey Joe

Drafting a Suppression Motion

YOU ARE WORKING AS an associate in an elite criminal defense firm. The firm has a reputation for aggressively pursuing all legitimate avenues of relief for its clients. Recently, you were assigned second chair in a big murder case. Your client, Joseph Tyler, has been charged with the murder of a man named Anthony Samuel. The police arrested Tyler, and incident to that arrest secured what is purported to be the murder weapon. You have been asked to draft a suppression motion seeking to exclude this evidence from the upcoming trial. In connection with that task, you receive a file from the partner who will take the lead on the case. That file contains the following documents: 1) an assignment memo, 2) the police incident report, 3) a witness statement from one Ronald Lamont, 4) a witness statement from an anonymous caller, and 5) the arrest report. Please review the entire file.

<hr>

MEMORANDUM

<hr>

TO: A.N. Associate

FROM: D. Partner

RE: Anthony Samuel Murder

<hr>

You will sit second chair during the upcoming trial of our client Joe Tyler. The prosecutor has charged Tyler with first-degree murder, robbery, a felony handgun violation and escape in connection with the shooting of Anthony Samuel. I will take the lead at trial. But, I am tied up with another jury case right now. I need you to take a look at some things for me.

Pre-trial hearings in Tyler's case are coming up. We need to draft the suppression motion. In the motion, we will argue that Tyler's arrest was unlawful because it was not based on probable cause. We will also argue that the murder weapon seized in a search incident to that arrest must be suppressed because it is the fruit of an unlawful seizure.

To give you some background, the police arrested Tyler on September 4 of last year when detectives saw him walking down Bateman Avenue. At the time of his arrest, Tyler was the key suspect in Samuel's shooting. The police did not have a warrant. I spoke very briefly with the arresting officer, Detective Jay Curtis, last month. It is his opinion that the warrantless arrest was lawful because he had probable cause. Curtis seems to think probable cause is established, in part, by the three statements he and his colleagues collected while they were investigating the shooting. Two statements were taken from witnesses who were at the scene the night of the shooting. A third statement was taken over the telephone a week after the shooting. These statements were produced during discovery, and I have attached all three to this memo. After receiving the statements, Detective Curtis and his team conducted further investigation. Based on their independent investigation, the police were able to confirm the truth of the following pieces of information from the statements:

1. Joe Tyler's middle name is Jerome and his nickname on the street is "Romie;"
2. Tyler lives at 1104 N. Calhoun Street;
3. Tyler has a cousin named Derek Wallis – Wallis' mother and Tyler's mother are sisters;
4. Wallis drives a two-tone (grey and burgundy) Toyota that is registered in his father's name – John Ragin;
5. The home at 1910 Division Street is leased to a person by the name of Stanley Nathan.

I assume based on the discovery we have received that the attached is all that was known to the police prior to Tyler's arrest. I need you to do an initial draft of the suppression motion. Please focus on the probable cause and search incident aspects. Also, please keep the motion short -- <u>no more than</u> 3 pages.

OFFENSE/INCIDENT REPORT POLICE DEPARTMENT	1. POD 7/3	2. COMPLAINT NO. 7H21235

3. TYPE OF REPORT Crime against persons	4. CONTINUATION OR FOLLOW-UP Follow-up	5. COMPLAINT/ VICTIM'S NAME (Last, First, Middle) Samuel, Anthony
	6. PAGE 1 of 2	7. CRIME/ INCIDENT Shooting/ Homicide

8. DATE OF ORIGINAL REPORT 8 Aug	9. DATE/TIME OF THIS REPORT 8 Aug 2351 hrs	10. TOTAL PROPERTY 1	11. LOCATION CODE

12. NARRATIVE: RECORD YOUR ACTIVITY AND ALL DEVELOPMENTS IN THIS CASE. INCLUDE ADDITIONAL VICTIMS WITNESSES AND SUSPECTS AS OUTLINED ABOVE. DESCRIBE DETAILS OF INCIDENT. DESCRIBE EVIDENCE AND PROPERTY AND INDICATE DISPOSITION.

In reference to this offense, upon talking to #1: Charles Mack, M-B 28 yrs of York St.,

and #2: Clotee Adair, FB-34 yrs of 567 Park Street, Mack and Adair conveyed to me

the following Information: that on 8 Aug. at approximately 2349 hours

the victim (Anthony Samuel) was waiting on the corner of Mosher St. and

Calhoun St. in front of "Louis Carry-out" located at 926 N. Calhoun St., victim was

awaiting Charles Mack to get off of work from the above-mentioned carry-out.

Mack then stated that as he went to talk to his friend (victim), Mack

witnessed a B-M — 20-25 yrs 5'6" 150-160 lbs wearing dark pants and a black

short sleeve shirt with the word "NIKE" printed on the front of the shirt, in white

lettering, walk up to the victim (Anthony Samuel) and subsequently grabbed same by

his gold rope chain which was around the victim's neck and at the same time

placed a dark colored, unknown caliber revolver to the back of the victim's head

and subsequently fired one shot, striking same on the right side of his neck just

below the right ear. Mack and Adair report that the suspect (30-1) then fled from this

scene with the victim's gold rope on foot south bound on the 900 blk. of N. Calhoun

St. Upon talking with #3: Ronald Lamont of 34 Downe Street (CON'T)

13. COMPLAINT NO. DISPATCHED UNDER OTHER THAN ORIGINAL	14. CLASSIFICATION		
15. REPORTING OFFICER (PRINT) SEQ. NO ASSIGNMENT Todd W. Etoner 17-887 WD	16. STATUS Open	17. REFERRED	18. TELETYPE NO.
19. REPORTING OFFICER (SIGN) ASSIGNMENT ADDRESS ZIP Todd W. Etoner WD 1034 N. Mount St. 54321		20. SUPERVISOR APPROVING SEQ. NO. Ofc. Grant Pratt A796	

OFFENSE/INCIDENT REPORT° POLICE DEPARTMENT		1. POD 7/3	2. COMPLAINT NO. 7H21235

3. TYPE OF REPORT Crime against persons	4. CONTINUATION OR FOLLOW-UP Follow-up		5. COMPLAINT/ VICTIM'S NAME (Last, First, Middle) Samuel, Anthony
	6. PAGE 2 of 2	7. CRIME/ INCIDENT Shooting/ Homicide	

8. DATE OF ORIGINAL REPORT 8 Aug	9. DATE/TIME OF THIS REPORT 8 Aug 2351 hrs	10. TOTAL PROPERTY 1	11. LOCATION CODE

12. NARRATIVE: RECORD YOUR ACTIVITY AND ALL DEVELOPMENTS IN THIS CASE. INCLUDE ADDITIONAL VICTIMS WITNESSES AND SUSPECTS AS OUTLINED ABOVE. DESCRIBE DETAILS OF INCIDENT. DESCRIBE EVIDENCE AND PROPERTY AND INDICATE DISPOSITION.

same reports that he saw 30-1 running from the scene of the shooting with a dark colored unknown caliber revolver in his possession.

Lamont also states that he then saw 30-1 run into an alley, in the rear of the "909 club" located at 909 N. Calhoun St. Lamont also gave this officer the same description of 30-1 as Witness #1 (Charles Mack). A canvass of the area was made for suspects with negative results.

The victims vehicle a 1987 Grand-Am gold/beige # 123M456 was taken to headquarters building 2nd floor garage by police officer John Howe, to be processed by the crime lab.

13. COMPLAINT NO. DISPATCHED UNDER OTHER THAN ORIGINAL	14. CLASSIFICATION		

15. REPORTING OFFICER (PRINT) SEQ. NO. ASSIGNMENT Todd W. Etoner 17-886 WD	16. STATUS Open	17. REFERRED	18. TELETYPE NO.

19. REPORTING OFFICER (SIGN) ASSIGNMENT ADDRESS ZIP Todd W. Etoner WD 1034 N. Mount St. 54321	20. SUPERVISOR APPROVING SEQ. NO. Ofc. Grant Pratt A796

POLICE DEPARTMENT

Statement of Ronald Lamont, taken in the homicide office on 9 August, by Sgt. T. McLarney

-- Began at 0150 Hrs.--

1. Q. What is your full name, address and D.O.B.?
   A. Ronald Sylvester Lamont, 34 Downe Street.

2. Q. Can you read and write?
   A. Yes.

3. Q. Are you presently intoxicated or under the influence of drugs?
   A. No.

4. Q. Please tell me what took place earlier on N. Calhoun Street.
   A. I was standing in front of ▮▮▮▮▮▮▮ talking to my friend Charlie Raymond . . . he lives at ▮▮▮▮▮▮▮ We heard a shot come from up the street, in front of Lewis sub shop. Then this young guy with a big gun came running down my side of the street and then across the street and into the alley that runs along side of the 909 club. Then some people were coming down the street saying that a guy had got shot.

5. Q. Please describe the guy that you saw running with the gun.
   A. He looked young, short hair and real light skinned. He had on a black t-shirt with ADDIDAS written on the front, in white. He had on long pants . . . but I wasn't really looking at his pants. He had this big dark gun . . . it had a long barrel. The guy was about my height or so, maybe 5'6". He was carrying the gun in his right hand.

6. Q. After reading this one page statement and finding it to be factual please sign it.

-- Ended at 0205 Hrs--

Ronald S. Lamont   8-9

Sgt. T. McLarney   9 Aug

POLICE DEPARTMENT

August 15

TO: Detective Jay Curtis
           Detective Richard James
           Homicide unit

FROM: Detective Ray McDonnell
           Homicide unit

REF: Homicide/Shooting
           VIC: Anthony Samuel
           H-8084

On 15 August at 0120 hrs. I received a call from a white female who did not want to give her name to me. She stated she had information about the Anthony Samuel homicide. She stated that a guy named Derek told his cousin, who she knows as Romie, to stick the guy up for his gold chain. She says Derek set the shooting up. She states that Derek's people live about three doors up from the old drug store in the 1100 blk. of N. Calhoun St. She says that Derek's mother's maiden name is Dianne Tyler, and that his father's name is Ragin. She states that the shooter, Romie, also stays on Calhoun St. She states that she thinks Romie has a bad eye.

She states that Romie went up behind Anthony and stuck a gun in his neck, and did not realize it was Anthony until Anthony turned and looked at him and said "cut playing," and that's when Romie shot him.

She states that Derek and Romie were standing on the corner in front of Old Fannies, and Derek told Romie to go stick Anthony up. She states that Derek sometimes drives his father's car which she describes as a little box type car with a burgundy top and a gray bottom.

This woman states that a guy known as "Markie," his real name is Stanley Nathan who lives in the 1900 blk. of Division St. is an eyewitness to the murder, and knows the shooter personally. She said a girl named Annie Wright who lives in the 800 blk. N. Appleton St. also knows all about the murder. Annie's mother is Alfea Wright.

POLICE DEPARTMENT

August 15

She describes Romie as being light skinned, and approximately 5'9" with a thin build. She states that Romie recently escaped from a prerelease center or some kind of work release program.

This woman states she knows all of this information because two of her nieces and her nephew were witnesses to the murder. She refuses to identify them because she does not want to involve them because she is scared. She states that she knows what its like to be a witness in a Homicide because she was one in 2007, she witnessed a murder in a bar and came forward, and subsequently had a nervous breakdown because of the stress she went through.

POLICE DEPARTMENT

Criminal Investigation Division
24 HOUR CRIME REPORT
78/151

From: 0500   4. Sept.   To: 0800   5 Sept.

To: Chief of the Criminal Investigation Division

From: Crimes Against Persons

Incident: Homicide/Shooting   7H-21235   H-8084

Location: 1401 W. Mosher Street

Time – Date: 8 Aug.   @2351 hours

Method: Victim shot once in right neck

Complaint or Victim: Anthony Avon Samuel, B/M/22, DOB 8-13-xx, 1412 N.

Mount St.

Suspect/s Wanted:

Arrested: Joseph Tyler, B/M/22, DOB 6-4-xx, 1104 N. Clahoun

St.

C.I.D. Investigator on Scene: Detectives Black, Kincaid, Young, Dyson, Vaught,

and State Police Corp. Stewart Russell

Summary: (To include records of Arrest)   ARREST OF SUSPECT

On this date, information was developed that the suspect
was staying at 2611 Garrison Blvd. Surveillance was set up in
the area and the suspect was observed walking in the 3400 blk.
Bateman Avenue. The suspect was arrested without incident and
transported to the Homicide Unit. A search incident to
Tyler's arrest was conducted and a .38 caliber dark colored
Smith and Wesson revolver was recovered from his waistband.
Revolver was ballistics matched to Samuel murder.

The suspect was interviewed and then transported to the
Western District and charged as follows:

First Degree Murder; Robbery; Felony Handgun Violation;
Escape

CHAPTER 6

Run Joe

Conducting a Suppression Hearing

YOU ARE WORKING AS a line attorney in the local prosecutor's office. Some months back, police officers in your jurisdiction arrested a young man on gun possession charges. Though the arrest began as a relatively routine matter, it ended with the young man, Jamie Blue, being severely injured. Specifically, Blue's spinal cord was almost completely severed. Doctors responsible for Blue's care explained days after his arrest that the injury would leave Blue a quadriplegic. Reacting to news of Blue's permanent paralysis (and expressing frustration over a spate of police-involved deaths or injuries around the country) your city erupted in civil unrest for several days. By the time calm was restored millions of dollars in property damage had been done, hundreds of people had been arrested, and dozens more were injured.

Notwithstanding the severity of Blue's injuries and the civil unrest following his arrest, your office has decided to proceed with Blue's prosecution. That decision was motivated by Blue's lengthy criminal history and the fact that the gun found on Blue has been linked to an earlier unsolved triple murder. The head prosecutor asked you to second chair the prosecution. The next court appearance in the case will be the suppression hearing. You have been asked to prepare a draft of the direct examination of the arresting officer. In connection with that task, you have been given just two items: 1) the Application for the Statement of Charges, and 2) a newspaper article detailing some of the facts surrounding the case. Please review and draft your direction examination.

(City/County)

APPLICATION FOR STATEMENT OF CHARGES
DISTRICT COURT

RELATED CASES:
....
....

00000 00001

COMPLAINANT	DEFENDANT
Ofc. Miller, G.	Blue, Jamie
246 West 29th Street	3703 Elmley Lane
AD 5907 J239	CC# 7-150404793

DEFENDANT'S DESCRIPTION: Driver's License # G-600-261-107-640 Sex: M Race: B Ht. 5-11" Wt. 195

Hair Blk Eyes Brown Complexion _____ Other _____ D.O.B. 8/12/xx ID Unk

Application for Statement of Charges

I, the undersigned, apply for statement of charges and a summons or warrant which may lead to the arrest of the above named Defendant because on or about 12 January at 1700 Block of Presbury Street, the above named Defededant (provide a concise statement of facts showing there is probable cause to believe a crime has been committed and that the Defendant has committed it):

Fled unprovoked upon knoti noticing police presence. The Defendant was apprehended in the 1700 Block of Presbury Street after a footchase. This officer noticed a clip-on handgun holster containing a handgun attached to the inside of his front right pants pocket. The defendant was arrested without force or incident. The gun was recovered by this officer and found to be a Beretta Px4 Storm Subcompact.

During transport to the Western District via wagon transport the Defendant suffered a medical emergency and was immediately transported to Shock Trauma via Medic.

I solelmly affirm under the penalties of perjury that the contents of this Application are true to the best of my knowledge, informatio and belief.

._____ 12 April _____.   ._____ G. Miller _____.

I have read or had read to me and I understand the Notice on the back of this form.

._____ 12 April _____.   ._____ G. Miller _____.

Subscribed and sworn to before me this 12th day of April _____.

Time: ____ 11:25 p.m. ____ ~~Judge~~/Commissioner: *A. Butael* _____ I.D. 1377

I understand that a charging document will be issued and that I must appear for trial when notified by the Clerk, at the Court location shown at the top of this form.

☒ I have advised applicant of shielding right.   ☒ Applicant declines shielding.

☐ I declined to issue a charging document because of a lack of probable cause.

DC/CR 1 (Rev. 12/2011) Print Date (03/2016)

(CITY/COUNTY)

Blue Arrested in Area Targeted by Police and Prosecutor

By Chris Julian· Contact Reporter

Jamie Blue has been left paralyzed for life after his encounter with police earlier this year. His injuries sparked civil unrest that left many neighborhoods in this city in flames. It was recently revealed that the significant law enforcement presence in the neighborhood was not simply Blue's bad luck. Weeks before Jamie Blue was arrested by police officers the office of the prosecutor requested significant surveillance of the corner where the chase began. The prosecutor, Jimmy Tucan, specifically asked the police to pay special attention to the neighborhood, and to provide enhanced enforcement in the area. This revelation could cause simmering anger at law enforcement to boil over once again.

In the weeks after the unrest, various news outlets have filed requests with the prosecutor's office for emails and other inter-office correspondence related to the Blue case. Emails released pursuant to those requests disclose that the division chief of the Crime Policy Unit at the prosecutor's office sent an email to the Police Commander weeks before Blue's arrest. In that email the division chief explained that his boss asked him "to pay closer attention to community concerns regarding drug dealing in the area."

The division chief also wrote in his email that the prosecutor's office wanted to augment previous successful crime reduction in the area by "targeting the neighborhood for more intense scrutiny by law enforcement."

Blue was arrested in mid-April. Police reports filed in connection with his arrest reveal that Blue was standing in the 1700 block of Presbury Street when two officers on bike patrol rounded the corner and saw him. Blue made eye contact with police before running away. The officers were dressed in standard issue bike patrol uniforms, and were riding standard issue police department bicycles.

Blue's doctors' determination that injuries sustained during his arrest would result in his permanent paralysis set off unrest in several neighborhoods. This unrest included arson, looting, and general rampaging that left property damage and human casualties in its wake. Calm was not restored for nearly two days, after the National Guard was called into the city.

Defense attorneys for Jamie Blue have complained that he was arrested long before police officers knew he had a gun. "Following a foot chase, Mr. Blue surrendered. He was then handcuffed at his surrendering location, moved a few feet away, and placed in a prone position with his arms handcuffed behind his back. It was not until that point that arresting officers found the gun." The prosecutor's office responded in a brief statement that "courts have long approved the involuntary detention of suspects—including the use of handcuffs—to investigate suspected criminal behavior."

CHAPTER 7

Say Yes
Negotiating a Plea

YOU ARE WORKING AS a Senior Assistant District Attorney in the prosecutor's office. Having been at the office for several years, you are now in a position to independently negotiate pleas in cases you are prosecuting without first clearing the negotiations with your supervisors. You are also authorized to approve plea offers for junior Assistants. You are required to keep the offers within certain broad guidelines. But, for the most part you are free to offer (or approve) the deal you believe to be most reasonable and fair.

The plea guidelines for the office are reflected in the following memo:

Memorandum

To: All Senior ADAs
Fr: DA Wallis

Thank you all for the terrific work you have been doing. We have managed to close a lot of cases in recent months. I am also encouraged by the fact that so many of the cases were closed with pleas instead of trials. The pleas you are hammering out save this office valuable resources and allow us to effectively manage the extremely high per-attorney-caseload caused by recent budget cuts and attrition. Your hard work is not going unnoticed. Thank you.

As you know, you are each authorized to negotiate appropriate pleas based on the particular facts of your cases. If you are the Calendar Assistant assigned to a particular courtroom, you are also authorized to approve recommended pleas by the junior Assistants in your courtrooms. In reaching settlements though, remember that the following guidelines apply:

> With the exception noted below, for <u>all</u> first-time offenders you may negotiate <u>any</u> reasonable plea (including assignment to the stet docket or the diversion track).

> You may not negotiate a non-incarcerative sentence for <u>any</u> defendant (including a first-time offender) if that defendant is charged with an offense that carries a maximum penalty of more than twenty years.

> If a defendant is a repeat offender, any negotiated plea must include some period of incarceration.

I know you are all aware of this, but in light of last week's disastrous across-the-board acquittal in the *Jeffers* case, keep in mind that in making plea offers you must factor in (and provide an appropriate sentencing discount for) the likelihood of an adverse suppression ruling and the likelihood of a loss on the merits under the beyond a reasonable doubt standard. If such discounting results in a recommended plea that falls outside of the above guidelines, see me to discuss. Keep up the good work.

Later that day, a junior Assistant in your courtroom approaches you to ask for approval of a plea offer. The Assistant is prosecuting a gun case. In exchange for the defendant (Jared Heinz) pleading guilty to the top count (possession of a weapon by a prohibited person), the

Assistant would like to offer:

- a ten-year suspended sentence;

- two years supervised probation; and

- a requirement that Heinz complete mental health counseling.

You ask the Assistant for the file and promise to get back to her the next morning. The file contains the indictment, a police report, and a signed witness statement. You review each of these items in turn:

**IN THE CIRCUIT COURT
FOR EVERY COUNTY**

```
STATE                          *     Ind. No. CCB-12-1234
                               *
v.                             *     (Felon in possession of a
                               *      firearm; Felon in possession of
JARED HEINZ,                   *      ammunition; Possession of CDS)
     Defendant.                *
```

****

INDICTMENT

The Grand Jurors of said county, duly called, impaneled and sworn to inquire, upon their oath do charge that:

COUNT ONE

On or about the 11th day of January, in the County of Every, JARED HEINZ did possess a firearm after having been previously convicted of a disqualifying felony on December 24, 2013.

COUNT TWO

On or about the 11th day of January, in the County of Every, JARED HEINZ did possess ammunition after having been previously convicted of a disqualifying felony on December 24, 2013.

COUNT THREE

On or about the 11th day of January, in the County of Every, JARED HEINZ did possess a controlled dangerous substance, to wit cocaine.

A TRUE BILL, Foreman of the Grand Jury

Next, you review the police report. It reflects that on January 11, the Crisis Hotline at the local hospital received a call from a man threatening suicide. The man identified himself as Jared Heinz, and told the hotline operator that he was "going to blow his head off" as soon as he hung up the phone. He was slurring his words and seemed to the operator to be under the influence of drugs or alcohol. When the operator asked what the tapping noise was that she heard, the man explained he was holding a .22 to his head and the gun was hitting against the telephone handset as he spoke. The operator could also hear a woman yelling in the background, "Jared, please don't. Oh my God, please don't do it." Heinz identified the screaming woman as his live-in girlfriend, Trish Malloch. But, Heinz would not let the operator talk to Malloch. The caller-identification information indicated that the call was coming from Heinz's residence at 1 Wallace Street.

The Crisis Hotline operator signaled to her co-worker to call the police. Officers Dumont and Etheridge responded to the call. Both officers were familiar with Heinz. Officer Dumont had twice arrested Heinz for threatening to shoot his (Heinz's) father, mother, and sister some years back. No gun was found during either of these earlier incidents and Heinz had been released both times without charges being filed. Officer Etheridge knew Heinz from several minor traffic stops. Both officers believed Heinz to be a dangerously unstable person based on their earlier contacts with him and based on warnings from other officers who knew Heinz as a violent man with a history of mental illness.

Before officers arrived at the Wallace Street home, a woman called 911. The woman told the 911 operator that her name was Trish Malloch, and that her boyfriend Jared Heinz had just called the Crisis Hotline threatening to kill himself. Malloch explained to the 911 operator that Heinz had since passed out in an upstairs bedroom; that he was no longer a threat to himself or anyone else; and, despite what he said to the Crisis Hotline worker, he did not have a gun and there were no guns in the house. Malloch insisted that there was no longer any reason for concern and apologized for the misunderstanding. When the 911 operator told Malloch that officers were already on the way, Malloch agreed to meet them outside.

The 911 operator related Malloch's message to Officers Dumont and Etheridge. Backup officers blocked off the street with marked patrol cars. Officers Dumont and Etheridge then proceeded to the house, where they met Malloch on the lawn. Malloch explained to the officers that Heinz was upstairs asleep, that there were no weapons in the house, and there was no further danger. The officers asked Malloch to wait where she was and pushed past her through the front door of the home, which was ajar. Dumont and Etheridge proceeded quickly upstairs, where they found Heinz sleeping in a bedroom. While visually scanning the room for weapons, Dumont saw a gun cleaning kit, but the officers found no weapon. They handcuffed the barely conscious Heinz and carried him to a patrol car. As Dumont and Etheridge secured Heinz in their car, two backup officers and a supervisor arrived at the house, and walked into the living room through the still ajar front door.

When Dumont and Etheridge re-entered the home after placing Heinz in the car, Malloch was sitting in the living room talking quietly to the supervising officer. It was not clear from the police report what the two were talking about. The supervising officer turned to Dumont, Etheridge and the two backup officers and ordered them in Malloch's presence to "for safety reasons, search the entire house for weapons." Malloch did not say anything.

The four officers fanned out to search the house while the supervising officer sat with Malloch. Etheridge began looking around the living room and saw ammunition in plain view on the floor, on a shelf, and on top of a television console. He did not find any weapons.

Dumont moved toward the kitchen, and as he was walking said to Malloch, "I'm going to look in here, okay?" Malloch did not respond. Dumont did not find anything of note in the kitchen. He proceeded toward a small laundry room just off the kitchen. As he stepped into the laundry room, he again advised Malloch, "I'm going to look in here." At this point, Malloch responded, "Okay." Dumont kicked several piles of dirty clothes that were strewn across the floor. When his boot hit something hard, Dumont reached down under the clothing and withdrew a loaded handgun. The other officers continued to search the home for approximately another hour but found no other weapons. They did however find a quantity of cocaine in the medicine cabinet in an otherwise empty pill bottle with Heinz's name on it.

Each of the officers quoted in the report described Malloch as being "very cooperative" and "extremely polite." The supervising officer indicated that Malloch even offered the officers something to drink at one point during the time they were in the house.

* * *

You also review the signed witness statement. It is Trish Malloch's. It confirms all of the details provided in the police report. The only additional detail it adds concerns Malloch's conversation with the supervisor in the living room. She described the supervisor as "nice," and explained that they were discussing the weather just before the other officers walked in.

* * *

Finally, you call the junior Assistant down to your office and have the following conversation:

YOU: *I am very close to making a decision on this plea offer, but I just want to confirm the statutory max on each of these charges. What's his exposure?*

ASSISTANT: *On the first count, Felon in Possession (Firearm), Heinz is looking at twenty years. On the second count, Felon in Possession (Ammo), Heinz is looking at ten years. On the third count, Possession of CDS, Heinz is looking at a statutory max of just five years because of the small quantity.*

YOU: *Are there any applicable mandatory minimums?*

ASSISTANT: *I thought there would be, but the legislature just did away with a bunch of mandatories to address prison overcrowding. So, no; odd as it seems there are no applicable mandatory minimums. If there were, trust me, I wouldn't be offering him such a good deal.*

YOU: *Why are you—offering him such a good deal, I mean? He's looking at a potential twenty on the gun charge alone. And this isn't a tough case to make. Even if Malloch doesn't want to testify, this is an open-and-shut case on just officer testimony. We could nail this guy, and they say he's dangerous. Why are you offering him no time?*

ASSISTANT: *Well, it's not no time, it's a ten-year suspended sentence. This guy can't keep his nose clean. He'll screw up in another couple of months and at that point he'll get locked up for the full ten. Plus, just between you and me, I'm not sure this is such an open-and-shut case. Heinz's lawyer is pretty sharp and I'd bet my next paycheck she's going to file a motion to suppress all of the* evidence—the gun, the ammo and the cocaine. I think they'll win it. This was a bad search.

YOU: *Are you kidding me?! A bad search?? I read the police report. The girlfriend consented. And even if she hadn't, the officers had a right to go in there without a warrant under exigent circumstances. He had a loaded gun, the Crisis Hotline operator heard it tapping against the phone. We can't just leave loaded guns lying around people's houses. What were they supposed to do, trust Malloch's word that there were no guns in the house?*

ASSISTANT: *No. They were supposed to get a warrant. They didn't ask for her permission to search and she didn't give it. Consent has to be freely and voluntarily given. Malloch didn't say anything related to the search until after there were five uniformed police officers swarming her house looking for a gun. Their supervisor ordered them to search and the only officer other than the supervisor who spoke to her didn't ask permission, he told her what he was going to do. Plus, the way I read this report and her statement, to the extent there was any exigency it dissipated when they placed Heinz in the police car. At best, we'll get the ammo in under plain view, but I'm not sure we'll be able to link it to him at trial; and my guess is the rest of this evidence is getting tossed by a judge. If we don't offer a pretty good deal on the front end, I think we're going to lose the case entirely.*

YOU: *I'm not sure I agree with you on this one. Even Malloch agrees that she said, "Okay," when the officer asked if he could search. She never objected to the officers being in the house even though she had ample opportunity to do so, and all of the officers described her as being very cooperative and compliant. She even offered them something to drink. If you don't want people in your house you don't offer them refreshments. But, I hear your concerns.*

*Let me think about this some more. At the moment, I'm inclined to
say I'm going to deny your request. I think a better offer—and one
that's more in line with our office guidelines—is a flat ten, plead to
the top count, we'll dismiss the rest. But, let me think about it some
more. I'll get back to you tomorrow.*

After mulling the case all night, you arrive early the next morning for
a meeting with the assistant before heading off to court. When you
call her office, you learn she's been pulled into a discovery conference
with a judge. To make sure you relay your message before she needs
to respond to the defense in the *Heinz* case, you decide to dash off a
quick memo to the assistant and leave it on her desk. In the memo,
explain clearly whether you are approving or denying her plea offer.
Be sure to include the reasons for your decision. If you are approving
her offer, do you need to talk to anyone else in the office before doing
so? If you are denying her request and instructing her to make another
offer in place of the ten-year suspended sentence she wants to give,
what is that offer and why?

 ## Points to Consider:

1. **Necessary Evidence:** In thinking about an appropriate plea offer,
one of your first steps should be to consider which pieces of physical
evidence are necessary to a conviction on each of the charges. Once
you have determined what the necessary evidence is, make a reasoned
judgment about the likelihood that each piece of evidence will be
suppressed. If necessary evidence is likely to be suppressed that
should inform your willingness to "sweeten the deal." If you believe
the defense motion to suppress will fail, that should inform your
desire to be tough.

2. Office Guidelines: Beyond the various statutory maximums, you also have a set of office guidelines that must inform your decision in this case. Are any of the guidelines relevant to *Heinz*?

3. Consent, Exigency and Plain View: Finally, recall what you know about the relevant exceptions to the warrant requirement that might justify the warrantless searches in this case. What are the factors that control each exception? Are those factors present here?

CHAPTER 8

Teenage Wasteland

Drafting Litigation Strategy Memo to Supervisor

IMMEDIATELY AFTER GRADUATING FROM law school, you landed your dream job in the Office of the City Attorney. You have now been in the office for just a few months. When you arrived this morning and turned on your computer, you found the following email from your supervisor, Sam Tyler:

To: You
Fr: Sam T.
Re: New Matter

I hate to pull you into a matter this complicated so soon; but, this is an important and politically-sensitive case. I need all hands on deck.

The mayor's sixteen-year-old daughter (Maria Z.) was stopped in the park last night while hanging out with friends. Police officers suspected the group (all of whom were underage) of drinking alcohol. The officers asked each teen to submit to a breathalyzer. The mayor's daughter and another kid passed and were sent home. Three others in the group failed, and were arrested.

The case has received a lot of media attention. The mayor, who was elected on a wave of small-government/libertarian sentiment, is complaining about the heavy-handedness of the police; and the daughter has threatened suit challenging the constitutionality of the police conduct.

There is an ordinance that governs this situation. Find it. In addition, please take a look at Officer Jeh Curtas' Incident Report. It contains the details we need. Once you've reviewed those two items, do some research. I need to know three things:

Did the police officers' interaction with the mayor's daughter implicate the Fourth Amendment?

If it did, did the officers need a warrant before asking the teens to submit to a breathalyzer?

If the officers did not need a warrant, what justification is there for their behavior?

Please draft a memo that addresses these three issues, and keep it short (no more than three pages) and clear. I'm ridiculously busy. Thanks, Sam

After receiving the email, you pull up the relevant statute. It reads:

B.C. Ord. § 10-57(d): A peace officer who has reasonable cause to believe a person less than 21 years of age has consumed alcoholic liquor may, without a search warrant, require that person to submit to a preliminary chemical breath analysis. The results of a preliminary chemical breath analysis or other acceptable blood alcohol test are admissible in a criminal prosecution to determine whether the minor has consumed or possessed alcoholic liquor. A person less than 21 years of age who refuses to submit to a preliminary chemical breath test analysis as required in this subsection is responsible for a state civil infraction and may be ordered to pay a civil fine of not more than $100.00.

You do a bit of additional legislative history research and learn that the statute was passed after a small group of concerned parents and teachers from the local public high schools expressed concerns about teen drinking. There was little evidence of any actual spike in such drinking (or an increase in any harm flowing from it), but the parent-teacher group expressed heartfelt concern about the possibility of underage drinking and the host of social ills that flow from it like sexual violence and other criminal behavior, declining graduation rates, and impaired brain development. Supporters of the statute also complained of the thirty-minute delay typically needed to secure a warrant if suspects were free to refuse a breathalyzer.

In addition, you pull a copy of Officer Curtas' Incident Report. The narrative portion of the report contains a complete description of the events leading to the teens' encounter with the police and the encounter itself. Based on your review of a couple of newspaper articles, the students do not dispute any of the facts:

INCIDENT REPORT

7:30 p.m., Friday: I was on duty in a radio unit with my partner. We received a call from an unknown motorist about noise and a possible fight in the park near the band shell. Upon entering the park, I saw an individual, later identified as Eric T., standing approximately ten feet from the park entrance near two idling cars. I also saw two parked cars further into the park, near the tennis courts. There were four individuals standing near the parked cars. Eric T. and the four individuals near the tennis courts all appeared to be under the age of twenty-one and two had on junior varsity jackets from the local public high school. We drove around, but found no evidence of noise or a possible fight. We also did not see any individuals near the band shell or in the park— other than the five individuals previously described.

Eric T. was still standing near the entrance to the park when my partner and I returned; but the two vehicles he had been standing near were gone. My partner and I alighted from our vehicle and approached Eric T. Our intention was to inform him the park was closing in approximately 2½ hours. As we approached Eric T., we smelled a strong odor of alcohol. We asked Eric T. if he had been drinking. He denied that he had. We also asked Eric T. if he knew the four people standing near the tennis courts. He responded, "Yeah, those are my peeps. We're just here roller-blading." After my partner read Eric T. his preliminary breath test (PBT) rights, Eric T. agreed to take a breath test. He tested positive for the consumption of alcohol. We placed him in handcuffs and in the back of our cruiser. We then walked over to the group of four individuals Eric T. said he was with. The teens weren't doing anything unusual, but in this officer's experience, when one teenager in a group is drinking . . . all of them are. My partner and I also wanted to see if the four had witnessed the noise and fight that were earlier reported.

My partner and I were in uniform and wore utility vests that said "B.C. POLICE" in reflective lettering across the back and over the left breast. Our service revolvers were holstered and we used a conversational tone as we approached. It was still daylight, though the sun had just begun setting. My partner instructed the individuals, who were later identified as Maria Z., Joy P., Derrick M., and Paul L., to have a seat on the curb and provide identification. Each teen handed over their driver's license. My partner ran each name for "wants and warrants" but nothing came back. As my partner returned the licenses, I knelt in front of the group to explain the park was closing in a couple of hours and to ask if they had seen anything while they were in the park that might explain the disturbance call earlier. As I bent down, I smelled a strong odor of alcohol. I did not see any containers of alcohol, and could not tell which of the four the odor was coming from. I read the group the same PBT rights card my partner read to Eric T. (attached), and asked if they would each mind taking a breathalyzer. One in the group, I don't remember who, asked what would happen if (s)he refused. I re-read the language from the PBT rights card explaining the teens could say no, but would be ticketed and fined up to $100. All four agreed to take the test.

Paul L. tested positive and was placed in handcuffs in the back of our cruiser with Eric T. Despite agreeing to take the test, Joy P. objected when asked to blow into the machine. She shoved the machine away, causing my partner to stumble backwards. My partner responded by placing Joy P. on the ground in a hard takedown. Joy P. continued to struggle and my partner had to apply pressure with her knee to Joy P.'s back and head to get her to comply. When the remaining individuals began getting unruly, I removed my pepper spray from my belt. However, I did not need to deploy it because they quickly quieted down. My partner handcuffed Joy P. and placed her in the back of the car with the other two. Maria Z. and Derrick M. took the test without complaint or objection and both passed. They were told they were free to go. The encounter with the group lasted no more than thirty minutes, though approximately ninety minutes lapsed from the time we drove into the park until the time we left.

The three arrested individuals were taken to the police station and processed, before being released to their parents.

PBT Rights Card

A Preliminary Breath Test is a test that analyzes the percentage of alcohol in your body.

- The test is conducted by you breathing into the end of a small machine.

- The test is not invasive and does not require anything more than a puff of air.

- The results of this test may be used in future prosecution.

- You have the right to refuse the request for a Preliminary Breath Test.

- If you refuse the test, you will be cited for that refusal and fined up to $100.

Points to Consider:

1. Application as a Prerequisite to Satisfaction: Be sure to recall the limitations on the Fourth Amendment's protections. You should always be careful to confirm the Fourth Amendment applies before rushing to analyze whether it has been satisfied. The amendment's provisions only apply under certain circumstances. Are all those circumstances present?

2. Application Revisited: When thinking about application, note the Fourth Amendment prohibits only unreasonable searches and seizures. Warrantless searches and warrantless public seizures on less than probable cause or reasonable suspicion are presumptively unreasonable. Did the police encounter here constitute either a warrantless search or a public seizure on less than the requisite level of suspicion?

3. Satisfaction: When considering satisfaction, ask yourself whether there are exceptions that might have authorized the police conduct. If so, what are they?

CHAPTER 9

Every Breath You Take

Preparing to Draft an Appellate Brief

YOU ARE WORKING AS an appellate attorney in your local public defender's office. Currently, you are working on the principal brief for a client who was convicted of various crimes related to the robbery of a Burger King. After reviewing the trial transcript and meeting with your supervising attorney, you receive an email from your supervisor that says the following:

> Great meeting with you. As we discussed, there is just one multi-pronged issue in the case. We will challenge the identification of the client by one of the Burger King employees. First, we need to argue that the trial court erred in admitting the witness' out-of-court identification, because that identification was based on an impermissibly suggestive photo array. Next, we will argue that the trial court erred in admitting the witness' in-court identification of the client where she did not have an independent basis for making the in-court identification.

At the time of the robbery two young women were working in the restaurant—one was a cashier, the other was a manager. After the robbery, both women gave a general description of their assailant to the police. However, it took approximately three weeks for the police to return to the store to present the women with a photo array. After viewing the arrays, the cashier could not make an identification, but the manager did. The manager identified your client. You have seen the photo array and believe it is impermissibly suggestive for a number of reasons—the client's picture is bigger than the other pictures, most of the other people in the array are noticeably older than your client, your client is the only one looking directly at the camera, and your client's clothing is different from that of the other men. Because the manager did not know the man who robbed the restaurant, you think there is also a strong argument to be made that there was no independent basis for the in-court identification.

If you are successful, a new trial will be ordered. However, perhaps even more importantly, without the identification evidence, the prosecution will be unable to retry the case. There was no physical evidence linking your client to the crime, and there are no other witnesses.

When you return from lunch, you have another email from your supervisor. This one says:

> I have taken a stab at drafting the Statement of the Case, and the Statement of Facts for the brief. A copy of the Statement of Facts is attached to this email. Can you take a stab at drafting the Argument section of the brief? You should limit your legal research to Supreme Court precedent and law from the highest court in our jurisdiction. Do not venture beyond these two sources of law (and do not utilize materials from any other portion of this book)!! Your argument section should be no longer than ten, double-spaced pages. Thanks a million.

STATEMENT OF FACTS

On December 5, the Burger King on North Avenue was robbed at gun point at approximately 6:20 a.m. (T1 146). Two teenagers—Kris Campbell, a cashier, and Sierra Middleton, the manager—were working in the store at the time. (T1. 147). Sierra Middleton was in the office, while Kris Campbell was out front, behind the counter. (T2. 18). A man walked into the store wearing a gray wool cap, dark sunglasses, and a green coat. (T2. 20). The man pointed a gun at Campbell and demanded money. (T2. 22). Panicked and scared, Kris Campbell called out for Sierra Middleton. (T2. 26). According to Miss Campbell, Sierra Middleton also panicked but eventually gave Campbell the keys to the cash register after dropping them several times. (T2. 28).

When Miss Middleton realized there was not much money in the register, she volunteered to open her own register and gave the man the cash in that one also. (T2. 28). The man took the money and fled. (T2. 29). The two teens then locked the doors and called the police. (T2. 29).

When the police arrived, Kris Campbell, the cashier, gave a description of the offender to the officers. (T2. 32). She described the man who had robbed the store as short, dark-skinned, in his late 30's, and wearing a green coat, dark sunglasses and a wool cap. Id. She also described the man as having a thick mustache and rough hands. Id. She said he "looked like he was on drugs." Id. Campbell also said the man had a gun that he pointed first at her neck, and then at her cheek, after grabbing her arm. Id.

Three weeks later, Detective Simon arrived at the Burger King to go over photo arrays with Miss Campbell and Miss Middleton. (T2. 30). The identification session with each teen was conducted separately. While conducting each session, Detective Simon put a piece of paper over the eyes and head of each man's photograph to replicate the hat and dark sunglasses worn by the man who robbed the store. (T2. 46).

Miss. Campbell's session was first. After going over two arrays with six photos on each sheet, Miss Campbell told the detective the offender was not in any of the photos she viewed. (T2. 38).

Miss Middleton's session was next. Just after the robbery, Sierra Middleton said all she could remember about the robber was that he was "dark, short, had a mustache and was wearing sunglasses and a green jacket." (T1. 148). However, three weeks after the robbery, and after Miss Campbell's unsuccessful session with the detective, Miss Middleton immediately identified the appellant, Lenny Robinson, as the robber. (T2. 47).

The photo array that was used by Middleton was admitted into evidence as State's Exhibit 1. In that array, while all of the photographs are the same size, Mr. Robinson's image is a "close-up," unlike the others. The enhanced zoom of Mr. Robinson's photo results in his face being approximately 40% larger than any of the other faces on the page. It is approximately 3 cm. tall and 4 cm. across. The smallest photo on the page is half this size. See generally (R. 3).

In addition, the direction of Lenny Robinson's gaze is unique. The other men photographed are not looking at the camera, they are all looking down and you cannot see their eyes. Only Mr. Robinson looks straight into the camera with his chin up. Id. In addition, while the other five men are wearing collared sweaters or shirts, Mr. Robinson appears to be wearing a basketball jersey or some other form of athletic gear. Id. Finally, Mr. Robinson is one of only two people in the array who clearly falls into the 30-35 years-old age group of the robber that was provided by Sierra Middleton and Kris Campbell. Four of the other five men are noticeably older—appearing to be in at least their late 60's. Id.

After reviewing the array, the trial court expressed some concern that the array emphasized Lenny Robinson's photograph. Specifically, the lower court stated, "I do note for the record, it does appear that one of the photographs seems to be a closer image than the other six. . . . The Court does find that number two is different from the others, and arguably suggestive in the showing." (T1. 174). However, the lower court ultimately found the array was not "impermissibly" suggestive and therefore allowed the out-of-court identification into evidence.

At trial, Kris Campbell testified, under oath, that the man who stood less than a foot away from her during the entire robbery was not in the courtroom. (T2. 31). In contrast, Sierra Middleton testified over defense objection that Lenny Robinson was the man who robbed the Burger King. (T2. 47). She also testified that when she identified Lenny Robinson in the photo array her words were "something to the effect of, this looks like the guy" and that she was "about 99%" certain of her identification. (T2. 50).

Sierra Middleton told jurors that the offender was not wearing a hat during the robbery, (T1. 148), while Detective Simon testified that Sierra told him the offender was wearing a dark knit cap and that it was Sierra Middleton who wanted to place something over the tops of the heads of the persons in the photographs due to the cap the offender was wearing. (T1. 165-166). On cross-examination, Sierra Middleton admitted she had never seen the offender before or after the robbery. (T1. 155).

There was no physical evidence connecting Lenny Robinson to the robbery. (T1. 49). And, other than Sierra Middleton's testimony there were no witnesses who claimed Lenny Robinson was the man who had been in the Burger King on the morning of the robbery. (T3. 16). Nonetheless, Lenny Robinson was ultimately convicted.

CHAPTER 10

Never Forget You
Making an Oral Argument

AFTER COMPLETING YOUR JUDICIAL clerkship, you accepted an offer to join the appellate division of Maryland's Office of the Public Defender. When you first received the offer, you were particularly excited because the office has a reputation for being a high-volume appellate office with seasoned attorneys on staff. You had visions of going to court weekly, and making brilliant arguments before the U.S. Supreme Court and the state's high court. Your day-to-day existence, however, has been a bit more mundane. For the most part, you spent your first year in the office reading trial transcripts, researching the law, and writing (and re-writing) appellate briefs.

Earlier today though you received word that one of your cases has finally been scheduled for oral argument! Pursuant to an order from the Chief Judge, time for oral argument has been cut to ten minutes per side. But, you are certain your brilliance will shine through in even that brief period. You can't wait!

In the case, your client was convicted of various crimes related to the robbery of a Burger King. At the time of the robbery two young women were on duty—one was a cashier, the other was a manager. After the robbery, both women gave a general description of their assailant to the police. However, it took approximately three weeks for the police to return to the store to present the women with a photo array. After viewing the array, the cashier could not make an identification, but the manager did. The manager identified your client. You have seen the photo array and believe it is impermissibly suggestive for a number of reasons—the client's picture is bigger than the other pictures, most of the other people in the array are noticeably older than your client, your client is the only one looking directly at the camera, and your client's clothing is different from that of the other men. On appeal, you are seeking to overturn the trial judge's admission of the manager's two identifications of your client (one out-of-court: the photo array, and one in-court: from the stand). If you are successful, a new trial will be ordered. However, perhaps even more importantly, the prosecution will be unable to retry the client without the identification evidence as there was no physical evidence connecting your client to the crime and there are no other witnesses.

Your case file contains your principal brief, your reply brief, and a brief summary of the state's argument. After reviewing the entire file, draft an outline of your oral argument and come to class prepared to present.

CASE FILE

In the Court of Special Appeals of Maryland
September Term

No. 014

Lenny Robinson,

Appellant,

v.

State of Maryland,

Appellee.

Appeal from the Circuit Court
(The Honorable C. N. Ellis, presiding)

BRIEF OF APPELLANT LENNY ROBINSON

Counsel for Appellant

TABLE OF CONTENTS

TABLE OF AUTHORITIES

STATEMENT OF THE CASE

Last July, Lenny Robinson was tried by a jury for his alleged role in the armed robbery of a Burger King (Case No. 206042), and armed robbery and assault of two Burger King employees, Kris Campbell (Case No. 206040) and Sierra Middleton (Case No. 206041). (T². 3). Lenny Robinson was ultimately convicted of seven counts in Case No. 206041, the case which identified Sierra Middleton as a victim. Specifically, he was convicted of 1) robbery with a dangerous weapon, 2) robbery, 3) stealing of less than $500, 4 & 5) first and second degree assault, 6) wearing, carrying and transporting a handgun, and 7) use of a handgun in the commission of a crime of violence. (T³. 8-9). In the case where Kris Campbell was named as the victim (Case No. 206040), Lenny Robinson was acquitted of robbery with a deadly weapon, and was acquitted of first and second degree assault. (T³. 10). He was found guilty in that case of 1) stealing less than $500, 2) wearing, carrying, and transporting a handgun, and 3) use of a handgun in the commission of a felony and crime of violence. (T³. 10). As to Case No. 206042, the case identifying Burger King as the victim, Lenny Robinson was found guilty of unlawfully stealing less than $500. (T³. 10). Lenny Robinson now timely appeals his convictions based on errors made by the trial court in the admission of evidence.

ISSUE PRESENTED

Whether the trial court erred in not suppressing Sierra Middleton's identification of Lenny Robinson where her out-of-court identification was based on an impermissibly suggestive photo array and her in-court identification was not supported by an independent basis.

STATEMENT OF FACTS

On December 5, the Burger King on North Avenue was robbed at gun point at approximately 6:20 a.m. (T[1] 146). Two teenagers—Kris Campbell, a cashier, and Sierra Middleton, the manager—were working in the store at the time. (T[1]. 147). Sierra Middleton was in the office, while Kris Campbell was out front, behind the counter. (T[2]. 18). A man walked into the store wearing a gray wool cap, dark sunglasses, and a green coat. (T[2]. 20). The man pointed a gun at Campbell and demanded money. (T[2]. 22). Panicked and scared, Kris Campbell called out for Sierra Middleton. (T[2]. 26). According to Miss Campbell, Sierra Middleton also panicked but eventually gave Campbell the keys to the cash register after dropping them several times. (T[2]. 28).

When Miss Middleton realized there was not much money in the register, she volunteered to open her own register and gave the man the cash in that one also. (T[2]. 28). The man took the money and fled. (T[2]. 29). The two teens then locked the doors and called the police. (T[2]. 29).

When the police arrived, Kris Campbell, the cashier, gave a description of the offender to the officers. (T[2]. 32). She described the man who had robbed the store as short, dark-skinned, in his late 30's, and wearing a green coat, dark sunglasses and a wool cap. *Id.* She also described the man as having a thick mustache and rough hands. *Id.* She said he "looked like he was on drugs." *Id.*

Three weeks later, Detective Simon arrived at the Burger King to go over photo arrays with Miss Campbell and Miss Middleton. (T[2]. 30). The

3

identification session with each teen was conducted separately. While conducting each session, Detective Simon put a piece of paper over the eyes and head of each man's photograph to replicate the hat and dark sunglasses worn by the man who robbed the store. (T^2. 46).

Miss. Campbell's session was first. After going over two arrays with six photos on each sheet, Miss Campbell told the detective the offender was not in any of the photos she viewed. (T^2. 38).

Miss Middleton's session was next. Just after the robbery, Sierra Middleton said all she could remember about the robber was that he was "dark, short, had a mustache and was wearing sunglasses and a green jacket." (T^1. 148). However, three weeks after the robbery, and after Miss Campbell's unsuccessful session with the detective, Miss Middleton immediately identified the appellant, Lenny Robinson, as the robber. (T^2. 47).

At trial, Kris Campbell testified, under oath, that the man who stood less than a foot away from her during the entire robbery was not in the courtroom. (T^2. 31). In contrast, Sierra Middleton testified that Lenny Robinson was the man who robbed the Burger King. (T^2. 47). She also testified that when she identified Lenny Robinson in the photo array her words were "something to the effect of, this looks like the guy" and that she was "about 99%" certain of her identification. (T^2. 50). Sierra Middleton also testified that she was "99.9% sure" she had looked at two photo arrays. (T^2. 54). But, Detective Simon explained to the jury that he had shown only one photo array to Sierra Middleton before she made her

4

identification, (T². 63); and there is only one photo array in the record that bears Sierra Middleton's signature. (State's Exhibit 1).

Sierra Middleton told jurors that the offender was not wearing a hat during the robbery, (T¹. 148), while Detective Simon testified that Sierra told him the offender was wearing a dark knit cap and that it was Sierra Middleton who wanted to place something over the tops of the heads of the persons in the photographs due to the cap the offender was wearing. (T¹. 165-166). On cross-examination, Sierra Middleton admitted she had never seen the offender before or after the robbery. (T¹. 155).

There was no physical evidence connecting Lenny Robinson to the robbery. (T¹. 49). And, other than Sierra Middleton's testimony there were no witnesses who claimed Lenny Robinson was the man who had been in the Burger King the morning of the robbery. (T³. 16). Nonetheless, Lenny Robinson was ultimately convicted.

ARGUMENT

I.   **REVERSAL OF LENNY ROBINSON'S CONVICTION IS REQUIRED BECAUSE THE TRIAL COURT ERRONEOUSLY ADMITTED TWO IDENTIFICATIONS— AN OUT-OF-COURT IDENTIFICATION BASED ON AN IMPERMISSIBLY SUGGESTIVE PHOTO ARRAY AND AN IN-COURT IDENTIFICATION FOR WHICH THE WITNESS HAD NO INDEPENDENT BASIS.**

Reversal of Lenny Robinson's conviction is required because the photo array used by the State was unduly suggestive and because Miss Sierra Middleton, the only witness to identify him, had no independent basis for doing so.

A.   **Lenny Robinson's Photograph Differed from the Other Photos in the Array Because of Its Excessive Size, Prominent Placement, and Singularly Unique Positioning of His Face.**

The Maryland Court of Appeals has laid out a two-step inquiry for due process challenges to out-of-court identifications. Jones v. State, 395 Md. 97, 109 (2006). At step one, the reviewing court must determine whether the identification procedure was impermissibly suggestive. *Id.* If the identification procedure was impermissibly suggestive, the court must determine at the second step whether, under the totality of the circumstances, the identification was, nonetheless, reliable. *Id.*

The Supreme Court has long recognized that all photo arrays present the danger that a witness may make an incorrect identification. Simmons v. United States, 390 U.S. 377, 383 (1968). The chance of error increases whenever the photo of the defendant that is shown to the witness is "in some way emphasized" over other photos in the array. *Id.* Indeed, "the degree of suggestion inherent in

6

the manner in which the prosecution presents the suspect to witnesses for pretrial identification" contributes greatly to a mistaken identification. <u>Stovall v. Denno</u>, 388 U.S. 293 (1967). Moreover, after an initial misidentification, the witness is "likely to retain the memory of the image of the photograph rather than of the person actually seen, reducing the trustworthiness of any subsequent courtroom identification." *Id.* at 383-384.

In the instant case, the lower court conceded that the photo array shown to Sierra Middleton was suggestive. Nonetheless, the court permitted the out-of-court identification (and never reached the second step of the analysis) based upon a conclusion that it was "not impermissibly so." (T[1]. 174). This ruling was in error. The actual makeup of the photo array left Sierra Middleton with little choice other than to select Lenny Robinson's photograph. <u>See generally</u> <u>Jones v. State</u>, 395 Md. 97 (2006).

In the instant case, Detective Alan Simon waited almost three weeks before showing photo arrays to Kris Campbell and Sierra Middleton, the two teen-aged girls who were working at the Burger King at the time of the robbery. (T[2]. 62). Kris Campbell spent the entire robbery in the robber's presence and was able to give police officers a detailed description of the assailant. Nonetheless, Kris Campbell did not see anyone she recognized in the photo arrays she was shown. (T[2]. 30-32). The detective then showed one of those same arrays to Sierra Middleton. Miss Middleton spent less time than Campbell in the robber's presence and could not provide a particularly detailed description of the man who robbed the store to police. Yet, three weeks after the robbery, and immediately

7

after Ms. Campbell's failed attempts, Sierra Middleton identified the middle photo in the top row (belonging to Mr. Robinson) as the photo of her assailant. (T². 54).

Her willingness to identify Mr. Robinson in the photo array was undoubtedly influenced by the fact that his photo was emphasized over the other photos presented. While all of the photographs are the same size, Mr. Robinson's image appears to be a close-up, unlike any of the others. The enhanced zoom of Mr. Robinson's photo results in his face being approximately 40% larger than any of the other faces on the page. It is approximately 3 cm. tall and 4 cm. across. The smallest face on the page is half this size. See generally (R. 3).

In addition to being a substantially closer zoom than the other images, Lenny Robinson's picture is also located at the top and in the middle. This prominent positioning of the photo calls it to the viewer's attention immediately. *Id.*

But size and positioning are not the only problematic features of the array. In addition, the direction of Lenny Robinson's gaze is unique. The other men photographed are not looking at the camera, they are all looking down so you cannot see their eyes. Only Mr. Robinson looks straight into the camera with his chin up. *Id.* His captured image appears confrontational and aggressive, while the other men appear docile or morose. Furthermore, while the other five men appear to be wearing collared sweaters or shirts, only Mr. Robinson appears to be wearing a basketball jersey or some other form of athletic gear that is further pronounced by the size of his image. *Id.* Finally, Mr. Robinson appears to be one of only two people in the array who clearly falls into the 30-35 years-old age group of the robber that was provided by Sierra Middleton and Kris Campbell. At least four of the other five men appear to be noticeably older. *Id.* All these factors greatly emphasize Mr. Robinson's photograph. As the Supreme Court recognized in Simmons this emphasis greatly increased the chances of misidentification by Miss Middleton. Simmons v. United States, 390 U.S. 377, 383 (1968).

Indeed, even the trial court recognized that the array emphasized Lenny Robinson's photograph. At the close of the suppression hearing the trial court stated, "I do note for the record, it does appear that one of the photographs seems to be a closer image than the other six. . . . The Court does find that number two is different from the others, and arguably suggestive in the showing." (T¹. 174). Yet despite this conclusion, the lower court found the array was not "impermissibly" suggestive and therefore never considered whether Sierra Middleton's identification could be considered reliable despite the suggestiveness of the array. This Court has the array before it. As a review of that array reveals, contrary to the lower court's finding the array was not just suggestive, but impermissibly so. See Hubbard, 395 Md. at 78.

> **B.** **The Out-of-Court Identification Should Have Been Suppressed Because Ms. Middleton's Identification of Lenny Robinson Was Not Reliable Where She Was Not in His Presence for Very Long, Was Not Paying Attention to His Face, and Did Not Identify Him Until Nearly Three Weeks After the Crime.**

For more than three decades, Maryland's highest court has recognized that the United States Supreme Court has fashioned a sliding scale of "taint" for out-of-court identifications and due process challenges. Webster v. State, 299 Md. 581, 600 (1984). On that scale, an identification procedure can be

1) suggestive but permissibly so, 2) impermissibly (unnecessarily) suggestive, 3) so impermissibly suggestive as to give rise to a very substantial likelihood of misidentification, or 4) so impermissibly suggestive as to give rise to a very substantial likelihood of irreparable misidentification. *Id.*; see Stovall v. Denno, 388 U.S. 293, 301-301 (1967); Neil v. Biggers, 409 U.S. 188, 198 (1972); Simmons v. United States, 390 U.S. 377, 384 (1968). Once an identification procedure is identified as impermissibly suggestive, the reviewing court must move to the second step in the process and determine whether a resulting identification is nonetheless independently reliable. To be independently reliable the prosecution must prove with clear and convincing evidence that the witness had a source other than the impermissibly suggestive photo array for the identification. Barrow v. State, 59 Md. App. 169 (1984).

In Neil v. Biggers, the Supreme Court considered whether an out-of-court identification that had been made under impermissibly suggestive circumstances was nonetheless reliable. 409 U.S. 188 (1972). The Court identified five factors to be considered in judging the reliability of the identification. Those factors include: 1) "the opportunity of the witness to view the criminal at the time of the crime," 2) "the witness' degree of attention," 3) "the accuracy of the witness' prior description of the criminal," 4) "the level of certainty demonstrated by the witness at the confrontation," and 5) "the length of time between the crime and the confrontation." *Id.*

Application the above standards in the instant case makes clear that Sierra Middleton's out-of-court identification was not reliable for several reasons. First

10

and foremost, she was not in the presence of the man who robbed the Burger King for very long. Indeed, Kris Campbell, who testified that Mr. Robinson was not the offender, was in the robber's presence far longer than Sierra Middleton was.

Moreover, during the limited time that Sierra Middleton was in the robber's presence, her attention was divided. She testified that her primary focus was on making the situation "end as quickly as possible." (T². 51, 53). She spent most of the time while she was in the presence of the offender not looking at the offender but rather talking with Kris Campbell, fumbling with her keys, giving Campbell the keys to the register, taking the keys back, and opening her own register. (T². 36-37, 45). Remembering the offender's face was understandably not Sierra Middleton's goal. Finally, when considering the reliability of Miss Middleton's out-of-court identification of Lenny Robinson, it bears mention that her review of the photo array did not occur until nearly three weeks after the crime.

Application of the Supreme Court's <u>Neil v. Biggers</u> five-factor test makes it apparent that Sierra Middleton's out-of-court identification was not reliable. In light of the actual photo array having been impermissibly suggestive and in light of the unreliability of Sierra Middleton's out-of-court identification based on that array, the trial court violated Lenny Robinson's due process rights in admitting the pre-trial identification evidence over the objection of defense counsel.

    C.   **The State Failed to Establish by Clear and Convincing Evidence That Ms. Middleton Had an Independent Basis for Her In-Court Identification of Lenny Robinson and, Thus, That Identification Should Have Been Suppressed As Well.**

After improperly admitting Sierra Middleton's out-of-court identification, the lower court compounded its error by allowing Ms. Middleton to make an in-court identification of Mr. Robinson as well. The Maryland courts have long recognized that where a photo array identification was obtained through impermissibly suggestive means and the witness does not have an independently reliable basis for making a subsequent identification, both the out-of-court and in-court identifications must be ruled inadmissible. Hubbard v. State, 395 Md. 73, 78 (Md. 2006). The State must show by clear and convincing evidence that the witness' in-court identification of the defendant had an independent basis. Hubbard v. State, 395 Md. 73, 78 (2006); Cook v. State, 8 Md.App. 243, 247 (Md. 1969).

In Hubbard, the Court of Appeals explained that the State must show the source of the in-court identification was the witness' observation of the perpetrator of the crime and was independent of the unreliable and tainted out-of-court identification procedure. Hubbard, 395 Md. at 78. In that case, the trial judge correctly suppressed an out-of-court identification because it was impermissibly suggestive. *Id.* The trial judge then allowed the State to call the witness in order to try to establish a separate and independent basis for an in-court identification. *Id.* at 80. The State failed to establish the independent basis with clear and convincing evidence and so the trial judge granted defendant Hubbard's motion to suppress the in-court identification also. *Id.* A similar conclusion was warranted in the instant case.

The identification of Mr. Robinson by Miss Middleton cannot be shown to be independent of the impermissibly suggestive photo array by clear and convincing evidence. Miss Middleton came into sight of the perpetrator only at the end of the incident. (T[1]. 147). In the few moments that Sierra Middleton was in the presence of the offender, she had a variety of other things she was focused on. (T[1]. 145-147). In addition, during the entire robbery, the man's face was partially obscured by a knit cap and dark sunglasses.

Indeed, the untrustworthy nature of Sierra Middleton's identification of Lenny Robinson is bolstered by the inconsistencies between her pre-trial statements and her statements made in court. According to Detective Simon, Sierra Middleton told the police that the offender was wearing a black knit cap. (T[2]. 59). However, in court Sierra was only able to remember that the offender wore a green coat with sunglasses. (T[2]. 44). In fact when asked directly if the offender was wearing a hat she testified that he was not. (T[1]. 148). By the time she testified at trial, Sierra Middleton could also remember only some of the details she had previously described about the incident. Moreover, she explained she had never seen the man before or since the day of the robbery. Under these circumstances, it is very unlikely her in-court identification was independent of the impermissibly suggestive photo array. (T[1]. 155). Accordingly, her identification is not rendered reliable as a result of prior knowledge. Cook, 8 Md.App. at 247 (1969).

*   *   *   *   *

The out-of-court identification of Mr. Robinson by Ms. Middleton should never have been admitted into evidence by the lower court. Due to its size difference as compared to the other photos in the array and the other ways it

13

emphasized Mr. Robinson, it was impermissibly suggestive and the trial court erred in not suppressing it. Without an independent source for her identification Sierra Middleton should also not have been allowed to make her in-court identification. The out-of-court and in-court identification by Sierra Middleton was the only evidence that the State had against Mr. Robinson. There was no videotape, no fingerprints, no other witnesses, and no recovery of the gun used. The conviction of Mr. Robinson must be reversed in light of the trial court's errors.

CONCLUSION

For all the foregoing reasons, Lenny Robinson's convictions must be reversed and his sentence vacated.

Respectfully Submitted,

Counsel for Appellant

Counsel for Appellant

SUMMARY OF APPELLEE'S RESPONSE BRIEF

1. The trial court properly denied the motion to suppress.

2. Although Robinson's picture is slightly larger than the others, that factor alone doesn't make the array unduly suggestive.

3. Because the array wasn't unduly suggestive, the analysis should end there.

4. But, even assuming the array was unduly suggestive, there are reasons to find that the identification was reliable.

5. Middleton had a long time (approximately 10 minutes) to observe the person who was robbing the store.

6. She also had undivided attention because the store had just opened and no other customers were inside.

7. Middleton did not have a gun pointed at her, unlike Campbell, so she was calmer.

8. Middleton was very certain of her identification.

9. For all these reasons the trial court's decision should be affirmed.

In the Court of Special Appeals of Maryland

September Term

No. 014

Lenny Robinson,

Appellant,

v.

State of Maryland,

Appellee.

Appeal from the Circuit Court
(The Honorable C. N. Ellis, presiding)

REPLY BRIEF OF APPELLANT LENNY ROBINSON

Counsel for Appellant

TABLE OF CONTENTS

TABLE OF AUTHORITIES

ARGUMENT

CONTRARY TO THE STATE'S CLAIM, THE TRIAL COURT SHOULD HAVE SUPPRESSED THE OUT-OF-COURT IDENTIFICATION BECAUSE IT WAS BASED ON AN IMPERMISSIBLY SUGGESTIVE PHOTO ARRAY

The State has argued that Lenny Robinson's photograph in the photo array "may be slightly larger than the others" but that "factor alone does not make the array unduly suggestive." See Appellee's Br. at 11. Lenny Robinson does not contend that the size of his photograph alone renders the photo array impermissibly suggestive. Rather, the photo array is impermissibly suggestive because of the five factors laid out in Appellant's brief that clearly distinguish Lenny Robinson's photo from the others on the page—size, placement, gaze, clothing, and match to description. When it comes to cases about photo array identifications, each case must necessarily be judged on its own facts. Menendez v. State, 146 Md. App. 23, 27 (2002).

The photo is indeed larger, and more than slightly. Lenny Robinson's face is approximately 40% larger than the five other faces in the array. His substantially larger face is also placed in the center of the top row. In addition, the gaze of Lenny Robinson as captured in his photo is different and unique from all five of the other men's photos. Lenny Robinson alone is staring directly into the camera. His chin is up and thrust forward and he alone appears confrontational and aggressive. Lenny Robinson's unique expression and gaze are even more pronounced in light of the size and placement of his photo. Four of the other men are clearly looking down, and all five appear docile or morose. These other men

4

are wearing collared sweaters or shirts of muted colors while Lenny Robinson

is wearing a basketball jersey or some other form of athletic gear which is again

even more easily recognizable due to the size and placement of his photo. Finally,

the two witnesses (Sierra Middleton and Kris Campbell) described the perpetrator

as being in his 30s; yet at least four out of the five men depicted in the array are

noticeably older.

Lenny Robinson does not argue that the size of his photo alone (or even any

of the other factors in and of themselves) makes the photo array impermissibly

suggestive. Rather, it is the combination of all these factors working together that

significantly distinguish Lenny Robinson's photo from the others. It is thus the

totality of the circumstances that renders the photo array impermissibly suggestive.

The State argues, in the alternative, that even if the photo array is

impermissibly suggestive, there is "ample evidence in the record demonstrating

the reliability of Sierra Middleton's identification of Lenny Robinson." Appellee's

Br. at 11. The State provides five examples in support of this claim. First, the

State argues that Sierra Middleton testified that the duration of the robbery was

approximately ten minutes. Appellee's Br. at 12. According to the State, this gave

Middleton ample time to identify the robber. However, contrary to the State's

assertion, Sierra Middleton actually testified that from the time she heard Kris

Campbell call her to the time the robber walked out of the store took "probably no

more than 10 minutes." (T². 45-46). Kris Campbell, who was the primary target

of the robbery, testified that the entire incident only took "about five minutes."

(T². 36).

5

The State next urges this Court to conclude that Sierra Middleton's attention was undivided because the restaurant had just opened and there were no other customers present. Appellee's Br. at 12. However, the record directly refutes the State's claim. There is no question the store had just opened. (T^2. 19). However, a review of the transcript makes clear that another customer was present in the store at least during the first few minutes of the robbery. Kris Campbell, the cashier, testified that a female customer had ordered and was waiting for her food when the man who robbed the Burger King came in. (T^2. 21). The customer remained in the store waiting on her food while Campbell and the robber had a rather lengthy interaction. It was only after the robber pulled out a gun that the woman made her way out of the restaurant. (T^2. 21). Moreover, the record does not support the State's contention that Sierra Middleton, who walked into the middle of this situation, had undivided attention. According to Campbell's trial testimony, Middleton was panicked (T^2. 28, 29), and was busy the entire time retrieving and handing off the register keys, taking the keys back and opening another register. (T^2. 28).

The State would also like to balance Kris Campbell's ability to take a close look at the robber against Sierra Middleton's in Middleton's favor. However, the transcript again contradicts the State's assertion. Sierra Middleton was most certainly in the presence of the robber for a much shorter period of time than was Kris Campbell. (T^2. 20-27). Moreover, during the entire time she was in view of the robber, Middleton was panicked, there was a gun, and as stated above she was very busy fumbling with keys and opening registers. (T^2. 28). In contrast, Kris

6

Campbell was able to have a a very calm and non-panicked look at the robber. This is because the robber came in and placed an order with Campbell well before the robbery actually began. (T². 22). Only after his order was placed did the man pull out a gun and ask for everything in the register. (T². 23). Yet, Ms. Campbell was still so unfazed by the request she told the man to "stop playing." (T². 23).

These were the circumstances—calm and even at times playful—under which Kris Campbell was able to observe the man who robbed the store. Under these circumstances, it is not at all surprising that immediately after the robbery it was Kris Campbell and not Sierra Middleton who could recall significant details about the robbery and the robber that Sierra Middleton could not. For example, Kris Campbell remember the man saying "kick that shit out." (T². 25). She also remember how far away he was standing, (T². 25); how he grabbed her arm, (T². 25); and how he pointed the gun at her neck and then at her cheek, (T². 26). Kris Campbell also provided a far more detailed description of the robber than Sierra Middleton could, including that the robber had a thick mustache, rough hands, and looked like he was on drugs. (T². 32).

Finally, the State has argued that reversal of Lenny Robinson's conviction is not warranted because Sierra Middleton testified that she "was 99% certain" of her out-of-court identification of Lenny Robinson. (T². 50). However, Middleton was also 99.9% sure she looked at two photo arrays with Detective Simon and we know that was not true. Detective Simon explained to the jury that he showed just one array to Sierra Middleton. (T². 63). Detective Savage's testimony is confirmed by the record evidence which contains just one array with Sierra

7

Middleton's signature (State's Ex. 1). Similarly, Middleton testified that she was "sure" the offender was not wearing a hat. (T[1]. 148). But, again we know she told the detective on the scene that the offender had been wearing a hat, and even wanted to place something over the tops of the photographs to replicate the cap the offender was wearing. (T[1]. 165-66). The fact that Sierra Middleton was "about 99%" sure of her identification, (T[2]. 50), cannot be given much weight in light of her similar certainty about facts we know not to be true.

A final factor established by the Supreme Court in determining the reliability of an out-of-court identification was not touched upon by the State. Neil v. Biggers, 409 U.S. 188, 199-200 (1972). Specifically, the Supreme Court has recognized that the length of time between the crime and the confrontation is relevant to an assessment of whether an identification should be admitted. *Id.* In the instant case, Detective Simon did not go back to show the photo array to Sierra Middleton for nearly three weeks after the robbery. (T[2]. 75).

Under the totality of the circumstance, there is no reason to credit Sierra Middleton's identification of Lenny Robinson as reliable. Consequently, where that identification was based on an impermissibly suggestive photo array and where she did not have an independent basis for identifying Robinson, the lower court erred in admitting her in-court and out-of-court identifications of him.

CONCLUSION

For all of the foregoing reasons, and for all of the reasons stated in his principal brief, Lenny Robinson's convictions should be reversed.

Respectfully Submitted,

Counsel for Appellant

Counsel for Appellant